DECISIONES

DECISIONES

A look inside at the legal battle between Salsa music legends *Willie Colón* and *Rubén Blades*, and an *Iraq War Veteran* caught in the middle, fighting for his honor and reputation.

ROBERT J. MORGALO

To my loving wife and children

CONTENTS

ACKNOWLEDGEMENTS

I WANT TO THANK SO many people for their support and encouragement throughout the five long years that I was embroiled in this legal battle. For those who took the time to listen to my story and to inquire with a genuine interest and objectively assessed the issues, I thank you.

I WANT TO THANK MY WIFE AND CHILDREN for putting up with my constant pursuit to clear my name—a pursuit that consumed me. You always provided the love and support I needed during the most difficult times.

THANK YOU TO MY MOTHER for demonstrating through her actions what true values are—values such as respect, humility, compassion, and love.

TO MY GRANDMOTHER for instilling in me discipline, strength, courage, and dignity.

TO MY BROTHER for always being there when the storms seethed and the battles raged, never leaving my side no matter the forces or the odds we faced.

TO JAVIER CERIANI, the only journalist to take the time to listen to my story, investigate it, and provide me with a platform for my voice to be heard. You and your team are true professionals. I am forever grateful for the respect and consideration you gave me.

TO MY EDITOR BARBARA FARMER. Writing this book was the easy part, but it was the painstaking process of combing through the thousands of words I have written, the long hours smoothing out the rough edges, fine tuning the message, and corroborating the source documents and supporting materials in order to produce a well-balanced and detailed final product. That was the hard part. Thank you for your professionalism and your enduring patience.

TO JAMES WOOSLEY OF FREE AGENT PRESS. Your expertise and guidance was instrumental in producing the final product and keeping all of us on schedule. You worked your tail off and delivered beyond what I expected. You are truly an expert at what you do. Thank you.

TO CARL GRAVES OF EXTENDED IMAGERY. You took a simple idea and book cover concept and made it a reality. Your work speaks for itself. You are a true professional and incredible artist. Thank you.

SPECIAL THANKS TO MY CLOSE FRIEND JORGE OLMEDA for encouraging me to write this book. Your friendship and support over the years has been a blessing to me and my family. Thank you, Jorge. I would not have written this book if not for you.

INTRODUCTION

WHAT YOU ARE ABOUT to read is a true story. It details an epic, five-year legal battle between salsa music icons Willie Colón and Rubén Blades and me, Robert Morgalo. The details of this book provide unprecedented access behind the scenes and an inside look into one of the most highly publicized and contentious court battles in Latin music history.

Before I go any further, I would like to make it clear that the assertions I make in this book are based on the evidence presented in the case, witness testimonies, and my own perspective. Everything here is supported by documents, statements, and evidence provided by the parties involved during the discovery process of this case. The appendix offers the exhibits and documents that were available as part of the proceedings. These documents, as well as all the works cited in the notes following the appendix, can also be found on my websites: decisionesbook.com (English) and decisioneslibro.com (Spanish). The documents will allow you to review firsthand the opinions and decisions made by the court that presided over the case. You can examine these documents and testimonies for yourself and draw your own conclusions about the evidence and the court's rulings.

I would also like to state that I hold no animosity toward any of the parties involved. Although the legal process was contentious and at times personal and deeply hurtful, I am satisfied that none involved were driven by malice or ill will; rather we each followed our own convictions and desire for justice, as influenced by our own perspectives of the case. At times, the actions taken by the parties in this case were deliberate and calculated based on legal strategies and tactics; at other times, they were reactive as a result of the unintended consequences of those same strategies and tactics. As you weave your way through this web of legal maneuvers, you will see that there were many opportunities to achieve amicable resolutions. You will also see that those same opportunities were often lost to pride and temerity.

Honor knows no statute of limitations.

Mark Twain

1

Place Your Bets

O N MAY 3, 2007, salsa music legend Willie Colón filed a
lawsuit against his former colleague and music partner,
Rubén Blades. The lawsuit was filed in the United States
District Court for the District of Puerto Rico.[1] In his lawsuit, Willie Colón claimed that Rubén Blades had breached a contract with
him; specifically, a promise to pay monies to him for a concert event
that took place four years earlier. That event was held at the Hiram
Bithorn Stadium in San Juan, Puerto Rico, in May 2003. It was
billed as a reunion concert with Rubén Blades and Willie Colón,
celebrating the twenty-fifth anniversary of the *Siembra* album, the
biggest selling salsa album of all time. The event was marred by

tragedy, gossip, accusations, and missing monies, and Willie Colón claimed that he was not paid for his performance as agreed. He further claimed that Rubén Blades assured him that he would personally be responsible for paying what Colón was owed; Rubén Blades denied this claim.

According to Willie, he had attempted to contact Rubén on numerous occasions to resolve the problem and was told repeatedly that Rubén was unavailable. Willie was forced to take legal action because his messages were ignored and he felt he was getting the runaround. He filed his lawsuit in Puerto Rico on the eve of the expiration date of the four-year statute of limitations, but since Rubén Blades was in Panama at the time of the filing due to his role as their minister of tourism, he was not immediately served. Whether Rubén was aware of Willie's previous attempts to contact him or not is unknown, but when the lawsuit was filed and the media reported the news, he was forced to acknowledge the issue.

During a press conference held in Panama in May of 2007 and later in his testimony, Rubén said he responded publicly because of his position as minister of tourism and because it had become such a highly publicized matter. He stated at the press conference, "They robbed me too. They robbed both of us."[2,3] He identified the individuals that "robbed" both him and Willie Colón of the money in question as Arturo Martinez and yours truly, Robert Morgalo.

Due to his statement at that press conference and his own unwillingness to respond to my numerous attempts to speak with him to clarify this matter, I decided to sue Rubén Blades for defamation. I figured that if he were unwilling to speak with me on his own accord, he would have no choice but to respond when presented with a lawsuit. I would have the opportunity to look him in the eye and confront him on his statements. He would have to face me and be held accountable for his accusations.

To be honest, I was angry. I was hurt. I felt betrayed and publicly humiliated. His statements at that press conference were carried on news outlets, tabloids, websites, and radio shows all around the world, not to mention throughout the Latin music industry where I had made my career. My reputation was severely damaged.

What made the matter most hurtful and personally wounding to me was the fact that Rubén Blades knew that as of January 16, 2003, I was no longer acting as president of the company that represented him for the past three years. I was no longer representing him as his agent, and I was no longer involved in any capacity with the business I had created, built, and operated since January 1, 2000. He knew I had been called to active military service for combat operations in Iraq with five days to report for duty.

On top of all this, I felt we'd had a close relationship. We did not interact socially or hang out with each other's families, but I did hold him in high regard. I appreciated his intellect and even felt a reverence for him. I expected him to have some consideration for what I was facing. I was given just five days to get all my affairs in order—to say goodbye to my wife and my children, to call my mother and father, to let them all know I loved them and reassure them that everything would be okay. The anguish and terror of leaving my family and going to combat without knowing if I would ever see them again was tearing me apart, but I could not show it. I had to be strong for them. I thought Rubén would understand this.

On March 8, 2008, I sued Rubén Blades for defamation. That lawsuit was filed in the United States District Court for the Southern District of New York.[4] I had no idea at the time that I would be fighting for my reputation for the next five years, and that during those five years, Rubén Blades would continue to make public statements through press releases and interviews that painted me in a bad light and further attacked my reputation and character. I was naïve enough to think that when he was served with the defamation law-suit, he would sit down with me to resolve the matter, that he would give me the opportunity to present my side of things. I was hoping for an occasion to provide the facts and information he might not have been aware of. I was hoping for the chance to clear my name. I had known him to be a reasonable man. Surely he would afford me that opportunity—but he didn't. Instead, I was met with resistance and more legal maneuvering. Those decisions set in motion a course of action that took on a life of its own. To be exonerated, I would have to fight for it.

In his song, *Decisiones*, Rubén Blades depicts the decisions that people make in everyday life and the consequences of those deci-sions. It's like placing a bet. We all have choices to make. Some are good; some are bad. Some will bring us joy, while others will fill us with regret. But whatever the case, there is always a lesson to be learned.

The account in this book echoes those same sentiments. It chronicles a series of decisions made by various characters involved in a legal battle fought in full public view. For better or worse, these decisions have impacted the course of their lives. Some fought for money, others for pride, and all for their own sense of justice.

But one fought only for a penny. You will find out later the sig-nificance of that penny, and by the time you finish this book, you will understand why a penny is worth more than a million dollars.

2

THE CASE

O N SEPTEMBER 11, 2001, terrorists attacked our country. By this time, I had been in the music business and also serving in the US Army Reserves for more than ten years. It didn't take long for the gravity of the situation to personally affect me. I was moved by what I was seeing on the news: stories of loss, of courage, of unification. I felt like I had to do something. I contacted Army Personnel Command and requested to change my status from inactive to active ready reserves. The following November, I reported to the 744th Military Police Battalion (MP BN) in Bethlehem, Pennsylvania.

At that time, I was president of a Latin music talent agency and concert production company called Martinez, Morgalo & Associates, Inc. (MM&A). We represented world-renowned salsa music artist and motion picture actor Rubén Blades and worked with many of the top Latin music recording artists in the industry. I created and produced the highly acclaimed Latin Nites at the Apollo concert series at the legendary Apollo Theater in Harlem.

Starting in November 2001, I served as an army reserve medic with the 744th MP BN one weekend per month while I continued to run my company. On January 16, 2003, a year and four months after the attacks, I received a WARNO from my unit. A WARNO is a verbal warning order instructing me to report to active duty while the actual paper orders were being sent. I received the WARNO with just five days to leave everything behind and report to active duty. My report date was my birthday, January 21, 2003.

Upon receiving my warning order, I contacted my business partner, recording artists that I worked with, and, of course, friends and family. I transferred all of the responsibilities of the company to my business partner, Arturo Martinez. I can't imagine the pressure he must have felt to be left with all the responsibilities of the business on such short notice. If he was experiencing those pressures, however, he did not let it show or express any concern for himself. Rather, his concern was more for me. That was just the kind of person Arturo was. When I look back, I see now that it was just too much for him. He was so good at dealing with the people and connecting with them—that was his thing. But he had little experience in the other business responsibilities, because that was my thing.

Given the short amount of time I had to say goodbye, I tried to contact as many people as I could. I know I reached out to Rubén Blades, but I cannot remember if we actually talked or if I just left a message. I know he knew I was leaving for war.

I was deployed to Iraq for combat operations, and I was gone for almost a year and a half. When I returned from Iraq on July 3, 2004, I found my business closed, a huge problem with Rubén Blades and Willie Colón, and my partner, Arturo, in prison.

As hard as it was going to war, that was easier than coming home. It was extremely difficult to say goodbye to my wife and children, not knowing what could happen to me. However, it is impossible to experience combat and come back the same. Integrating back into normal life is severely hindered by scars of war. I was a shell of the person I had been before—I was broken by the experiences, the sights, the sounds, the smells. I had left combat, but combat didn't leave me.

When I returned, I was in no shape to handle any problems with the business. I discovered the massive financial problem with the May 2003 reunion tour in Puerto Rico concerning Willie and Rubén, but on top of that, my partner had been caught smuggling cocaine into the United States from Panama in order to get extra cash to deal with the lost money. He was sentenced to fifteen years in prison. How was I to deal with all of this?

In 2007, Willie Colón sued Rubén Blades and an intense legal battle began—a legal battle that dragged me into an ordeal I had nothing to do with. I stood accused of stealing money from both Rubén and Willie, although Willie always maintained that I'd had no involvement. It was Rubén Blades who accused me, and he did so publicly. That is why I sued Rubén Blades for defamation.

By the time the case went to trial, my ex-partner, Arturo, having served five years of his fifteen-year sentence, was working with or for Rubén Blades along with some other people who were involved either directly or indirectly with the events in question. They were now Rubén's star witnesses, and they were all testifying against me.

This is the story of that case.

3

CAST OF CHARACTERS

IN ORDER TO BETTER appreciate the controversies and dynamics of this legal drama, it is important to meet the main characters and supporting cast members, as well as to understand each one's involvement.

Willie Colón and Rubén Blades are without a doubt the main protagonists here. Without these two leading men, there would be no story to tell. Rubén Blades is a composer, actor, singer, politician, activist, and academic scholar. He has received many awards and recognitions in his distinguished career. He has won numerous Grammy Awards and has been in more than forty major motion pictures and television shows. He is a one-time presidential candidate for

Panama, a Harvard Law School graduate, and a former United Nations goodwill ambassador.

Likewise, Willie Colón has had a successful and highly accomplished career. He is a composer, producer, political activist, politician, musician, and bandleader. He is one of the biggest sellers in his genre with over forty productions and more than thirty million records sold worldwide. He has garnered eleven Grammy nominations, a lifetime achievement award from the Latin Academy of Recording Arts and Sciences, and fifteen gold and five platinum albums.

Together, Willie Colón and Rubén Blades set the bar for record sales with their most famous production to date, *Siembra*, which is still one of the biggest selling albums in the history of its genre. It is this album that is at the heart of this case. It is what defined their place in Latin music history. It is what brought these two music legends together in a way that even their own accomplished solo careers could not escape. Yet, it was ultimately the foundation upon which their bond was irreconcilably severed. Willie Colón and Rubén Blades' long-lasting public and private love/hate relationship has existed for as long as their musical talents first crossed paths. That is why the *Siembra* reunion show was such a big deal.

In supporting roles to this drama, we have Ariel Rivas and Arturo Martinez. Ariel Rivas is a concert promoter and artist manager who was the producer of the twenty-fifth anniversary concert for the *Siembra* album. He played an integral part in the events that transpired before and after the *Siembra* concert and was a witness called to testify by Rubén at trial. Prior to the *Siembra* concert, Ariel Rivas had never worked with Rubén Blades. But as things turned out, the chaos that ensued in the aftermath of that now infamous concert created an opportunity for Ariel to position himself as one of Rubén Blades' current representatives.

Arturo Martinez was my business partner, my friend, and closest confidant. He was vice president of Martinez, Morgalo & Associates. I founded the company in December of 1999, and brought him in as partner in March of 2000. When I incorporated the company, I asked him to join me, and I gave him 49 percent ownership. We flipped a coin to see whose name would go first. During the three years we ran the company together, I counted on Arturo Martinez to travel with the artists we represented. He had a great temperament, and his likable demeanor with the artists and promoters made it easy to deal with him. Arturo was rough around the edges, but he had a heart of gold. He was liked by just about everyone. He was not a highly educated man, but he was street-smart and genuine. He was a street hustler who knew how to get things done and make connections, but he lacked business savvy. He was no dummy, but he was not familiar with how to run a business. Sometimes his street personality would be an asset and other times a potential liability. For example, one night we had a party to celebrate the opening of our office. It was the debut of the business and an official announcement of our representation of Rubén Blades. A lot of media and industry people were there. Danny Glover, who had worked on two movies with Rubén, even stopped by. I was not much for all-nighters, so I left the party early. When I got into the office the next morning, I learned that Arturo had beaten up someone for stealing CDs out of a musician's bag. Although I knew why he did it and even empathized, I explained to him that we owned a company now, and his actions could lead to a lawsuit against what we were trying to build. I told him we had to be professional in our actions. He understood, apologized, and it never happened again.

The final cast member in this ordeal is me. Every story has a villain. In this case, if you believe what has been said in the media, I am the villain. No, I am not admitting any wrongdoing. I am just "playing the part" that was given me—a character cast so prominently in this tale that it has become nearly impossible for the audience to discern the role I was given from the person I truly am. I have been—as it's commonly called in the industry—typecast. Once someone is typecast, it is difficult to break free from that role. My hope in sharing this story is to allow you, the reader, to see for yourself what I was fighting for and to judge in your own mind what part I played in this drama.

4

GROWING UP

NOW THAT YOU HAVE met the cast, I would like to fill you in on my background and the paths that have taken me from humble beginnings to a feature on the cover of *Billboard* magazine; from a war zone in Iraq to an epic legal battle back home.

I won't bore you with all the details of my early life, but I will give you some basic information that will help you better understand who I am and how I got here. My parents came to America as refugees from Cuba. My dad left my mother when I was ten months old. My mother and grandmother raised my brother and me in Miami, Florida. My mother worked two jobs to keep food on the table and a roof over our heads. My grandmother was tough as nails and taught us how to clean, make our beds, climb trees, and fight. She never let us take the easy road and never let us back down from a fight. Discipline was never in short supply. She taught us the value of hard work and standing up for ourselves. She also taught us to be thankful for the opportunities this country had given us. She instilled in us a love of country and a sense of patriotism. She taught us that every job is honorable, whether a garbage man or a businessman, so long as it is done with integrity.

My brother, who is a year and one month older than I am, quit school when he was sixteen to get a job in order to help our mother with the bills. He joined the army when he was seventeen and served in the infantry. He was and still is my biggest supporter. I am his little brother, no matter how old I get. No matter what troubles come my way or what jams I find myself in, he is always there by my side. He has never let me down. He has always been right there with me.

When I was sixteen, I followed in my brother's footsteps, also quitting school. However, it wasn't until I was twenty-three that I joined the US Army Reserves. I had no clue that that decision to join in 1989 would have such an impact on my life more than twenty-five years later. I had no idea that I would eventually retire from the army, a disabled veteran. Nor did I know that what started as a curiosity in the music business would turn out to be a successful career, or that it would run parallel with my service in the Army Reserves and ultimately come to an end as a casualty of that service.

5

RIGHT PLACE, RIGHT TIME

ONE COULD EASILY ARGUE that my career in the music business was either the product of pure luck or destined by fate. But there is absolutely no doubt in my mind that it was a specific moment in time, a chance encounter, the proverbial "being at the right place at the right time," that set me on the path that would define my life and create my history—a journey of unexpected achievements, accomplishments, and joy, as well as epic failures, struggles, and loss.

It was 1985. I was nineteen years old, a high school dropout, jumping from one menial, minimum wage job to another. I was a floater. Floating through life without a care in the world, with no responsibilities, no direction, and completely clueless. I had no vision, no purpose, no ambitions, and most importantly, no confidence in myself. I was resolved to live an unremarkable life, never to amount to much. I lived for the moment, and thoughts of the future never took up residence in my mind. The future was as much a nomad as I was.

All my friends had something going on at the time. They were either in college or carrying on with their family business or working in good paying jobs. I was "that guy." The tagalong. The guy who slept on your couch, ate at your parent's house, and borrowed more money than he could ever repay. Every Friday or Saturday night, my friends and I would meet up at the grocery store parking lot to decide what we were going to do that night. Sometimes we would go to the bowling alley or pool hall. Other times we would crash a party or go to a club.

On one particular Friday in February 1985, all my friends had tickets to go to an Iron Maiden/Twisted Sister concert at the Hollywood Sportatorium in Pembroke Pines, Florida. Back then there was no Internet or buying tickets online. If you wanted to get good seats for a concert, you camped out all night outside of Specs or some other music store to get your tickets. Since I was always living in the moment, I didn't have a ticket. In fact, I had never been to a concert. This was just not something I did, due to lack of money and never knowing where I would be at any given point in time. But this time, I decided not having a ticket was not going to stop me. I was not going to be left out on a Friday night with nothing to do and no one to hang out with. I was going even if I had to sneak in, scalp a ticket, or just hang around outside. I didn't have much going for me, but one thing I did have was a go-for-it attitude that didn't know the meaning of "can't." This was something that would fuel my life and my endeavors. You will see this character trait over and over again in the chapters to come. I've never been afraid to go for it, even when I was clearly out of my league or way over my head. I don't know if this is due to courage, determination, or a need to prove something to myself.

When we arrived at the Hollywood Sportatorium, I was amazed at all of the people who were there. The energy and excitement could be seen and felt even in the parking lot as we walked toward the box office. Luckily, there were still tickets available, and I was able to purchase one. I must have just gotten paid, because having cash in my pocket only happened on payday. I was usually broke the very next day. I think I paid fifteen dollars for that ticket. We entered the concert venue, but while my friends were way up front, I was seated all the way back in the nosebleed section.

I don't think I saw much of the concert. I was just amazed at the number of people, the production, the sights and sounds, the smell (weed was prevalent), and the excitement I was feeling. How did this all work? How does something like this happen? Who puts this together? I paid fifteen dollars for my ticket; how many people are here? How much money is made? Where does all the money go? I had so many more questions. The answers would not come until several years later, but one thing was certain that night. What I experienced at that concert started something in me that was beyond my control. It was greater than me and my capacity and my resources. I don't know exactly what was triggered in me that night, but it was undeniable.

Fast-forward three years. My friends were part-time garage band musicians. They did not do it to play gigs or become rock stars. They just did it for the music, for fun, and it was a great opportunity to hang out. We would all get together at a local rehearsal studio to jam out. I was not in the band. I couldn't play an instrument, nor could I sing, but I knew deep in my heart that if I had any talent at all, I would be dangerous because even without any talent, I was entertaining and unafraid to make a spectacle of myself. I was the funny man, the jokester, the clown. I helped with the setup and tagged along just as I always did.

One night, the guys were all arguing and pissed off. They were upset because the rehearsal studio was raising its studio time fees from fifteen to twenty dollars per hour. My best friend Jesus (the drummer) and I loaded his drums into the van and talked about it on our way home from the rehearsal. I couldn't understand what the big deal was. There were five guys in the band, and the difference in price boiled down to only one dollar more per hour per musician. I told Jesus, "We should open our own studio." He looked at me like a lightbulb had lit up inside his brain and was gleaming out through his eyes. I will never forget that look.

I didn't have any money, but I had started going to college and was receiving financial aid and student loans. Since I had no real expenses due to my floater status, I was able to use that student loan money to go into business with Jesus. We opened Proto Productions. He came up with the name, and I didn't care. We rented a warehouse in Doral, Florida, that served a triple purpose. Part of it was used for his family textile business, which was growing too big to keep it working out of their home garage; another part was allocated for the rehearsal studios (we had two soundproof rooms built in the warehouse); and just above the main office of the warehouse, we set up a room for me to live in. It had no shower, but I had a place of my own for the time being.

Around this time, I started working as an admissions counselor at Saint Thomas University in North Miami, Florida. How I got that job is beyond me. I had no idea what the job entailed, and I had only a GED education with about nine college credits to my name. Nevertheless, there I was, helping people navigate through their college decisions and working toward recruiting new students for the school. Saint Thomas is a private university. It was going through a budget crunch at the time, and I had the bright idea of putting together a benefit concert to help raise funds. What the hell was I thinking? I had no knowledge of how to go about it and was probably delusional in thinking I could replicate what I had experienced at that concert a few years before. But once again, that go-for-it attitude prevented me from setting any limits for myself. Not knowing how to do it was not going to stop me from trying. I had nothing to lose.

I grabbed hold of my record collection and pulled out Stevie Ray Vaughan's *Couldn't Stand the Weather* album. I pulled the vinyl record out of its sleeve and looked to see where it was made—New York City. I called information and asked for the phone number of the record label in New York. They gave me the number, and I called the company.

The conversation went something like this:

> Me: Hi, I am interested in doing a benefit concert. How do I go about getting Stevie Ray Vaughan for a concert?
>
> Record Label: Oh, you want booking information.

I wrote that down: "booking information." I didn't even know what it meant. They gave me the telephone number for International Creative Management (ICM). So I called them, and that call went something like this:

> Me: Hello, I would like booking information on Stevie Ray Vaughan, please.

I was learning the lingo as I went along.

> ICM: Where are you calling from?
>
> Me: Miami, Florida.
>
> ICM: Let me get you to the responsible agent.

I wrote down "responsible agent," and was transferred to the booking department.

> Me: Hi. I would like to speak with the responsible agent for Stevie Ray Vaughan for booking information please.

I was practically an expert.

> Booking: Where are you calling from?
>
> Me: Miami, Florida.
>
> Booking: Hold on.

They connected me with the responsible agent's assistant.

> Assistant: How can I help you?
>
> Me: Yes, I am interested in booking information for Stevie Ray Vaughan and the Fabulous Thunderbirds for a benefit concert at Saint Thomas University.

I was getting bold now.

> Assistant: Have you ever done this before?

He must have realized I did not know what the hell I was doing.

> Me: No...but...I want to get them together for a
> concert—

He didn't even let me finish. He dug into me and spoke to me like I was his bitch. He humiliated me and made me feel like a worthless piece of shit. I was embarrassed and speechless. I just sat there at the point of tears, being belittled and degraded by the assistant of some responsible agent. I hung up and sat there for a while longer. I was shaken. I was hurt. I was insecure. Then I was mad. Who the hell was this guy to talk to me like that? I was beyond angry. Now, I was on a mission.

After composing myself from the brutal verbal abuse I'd received from the agent at ICM, I grabbed another record. This time it was B. B. King. By now it should be clear that I love the blues. Maybe that's why I was such a glutton for pain and suffering. I went through the same process as before—calling information, asking for the record company telephone number, getting the booking agency information, and requesting to speak with the responsible agent. It all seemed second nature by now. I was in a groove and not deterred in any way by the blistering burns from my last attempt. This time I was not going to be anyone's bitch. I was given the number for the Associated Booking Agency. I made contact with the responsible agent, a guy by the name of Ken Lesnick.

To my surprise, Ken Lesnick was respectful and not at all what I had encountered with ICM. He was a little arrogant in the sense that he wanted to screen me to see if I was serious. I spoke with more confidence now and presented myself as someone with both experience and an equally arrogant persona. I told him I was interested in booking B. B. King for a gig in Miami, Florida. He asked me if I had promoted any events and what company I was with. I spit out a bunch of names and events and told him I was with Hot Miami Productions. Although I did eventually incorporate Hot Miami Productions in 1989, there was no such company at the time, and I had never done any of the events I told him about. He never drilled me on them, but I'm pretty sure he was not all that convinced I was telling him the truth. I guess maybe it was my boldness that kept him engaged and/or amused. He was not willing to give me a date with B. B. King. Instead he was pushing Bobby "Blue" Bland on me. I didn't know much about Bobby Bland at the time, so I kept pushing for B. B. King.

During the same time that I was inquiring and negotiating for the B. B. King date, I was also researching the costs involved with renting the James L. Knight Center in downtown Miami, as well as advertising costs for radio, television, and newspapers. I made contact with a guy by the name of Manny (I can't remember his last name, but I think it was Rodriguez). He was the facility manager of the James L. Knight Center. I told him I was interested in promoting a concert there with B. B. King and Bobby Blue Bland. He was very cooperative and helped me understand the process and costs involved to rent the theater. I was surprised to find the rental fee was only $2,500. This was a five-thousand-seat venue where many concerts took place. I expected it to be much more expensive. Then Manny explained to me that the rental was just for the theater and did not include other charges such as ushers, box office, security, sound, lights, and other related costs. But he gave me enough information for me to get a clearer picture of what needed to be done and how much it would cost.

If I recall correctly, Ken Lesnick told me that the artist fee or "guarantee" for B. B. King was about $25,000 plus all rider requirements, and Bobby Bland was $5,000 plus all rider requirements. I said no problem and that I would get back to him. Then I called Manny and ask him what a rider requirement was. He explained to me that a rider was like an addendum to a performance contract that includes particular requirements that the artists call for, such as sound requirements, hotel rooms, ground transportation, dressing room requirements, on-call doctors, and so on. Then I called Ken and told him to send me the rider to look at. He told me to send him an offer, and I did. I didn't know how to submit an offer, but I did my best. The only thing I remember is that I spelled "rider" like the truck rental company. So my offer was $25,000 plus all Ryder requirements for B. B. King and $5,000 plus all Ryder requirements for Bobby Blue Bland.

The deal was struck. I hung up and was so excited. I couldn't believe it. I did it! I got it done. Then reality set in. I didn't have any money. *What a great deal,* I thought. *But now what? What do I do?* So I put together a profit-and-loss sheet with all of the known expenses and a scale of all probable sales potential from a loss to a sell out and what the break-even point would be. After that, I presented it to anyone who was willing to listen and had the resources to invest. At the end of the day, it was a great experience. I found the investors, and the rest, as they say in the music industry, is history.

6

THE NEW GROOVE

FTER LAUNCHING MYSELF INTO the business, I started producing festival-style concerts and events. The first festival I produced was called Liberty Fest '89. It was a jazz concert at the Bayfront Park Amphitheater, featuring Nestor Torres as the headliner, Ed Calle and Dreadfull Rhythm as support acts. This event took place on Fourth of July weekend in 1989.

Around the same time that I started playing around with the music business, I realized I needed to do something more with my life. I had just received fifteen W2s for tax purposes for one year. That's more W2s than there are months in the year! I needed to figure something out. So in November 1989, I decided to enlist in the

US Army National Guard. I ended up scoring very well on the ASV-AB test (Armed Services Vocational Aptitude Battery) and literally had my choice of any job the army had to offer. When the vocational counselor told me I could be a medic, something clicked. Until that moment, I never imagined that kind of work could be an option for me. So I took it. As it turns out, I excelled in the army. I had never been pushed to my full potential before. I'd just been a loser getting by in life. But I overcame all of the challenges and obstacles that the drill sergeants threw at me, and I graduated with honors from AIT (Advanced Individual Training). I ended up being in the army reserves for as long as I was in the music business.

In 1991, I produced Liberty Fest '91 with Mickey Gilley, Jerry Reed, and Tom T. Hall. It was another Fourth of July celebration, inaugurating a new baseball sports complex in Homestead, Florida. We had just won the Gulf War, and I thought it was an appropriate time to get back into the business after returning from basic training and AIT as a combat medic. There are too many concerts and events to name with any specificity after that, but over the next few years I produced events with the Temptations, Wolfman Jack, the Spinners, the Russell Simmons' Def Comedy Jam, and many more.

In 1992, I moved to Orlando, Florida. While I was there, I saw an opportunity to start producing Latin music. Until now, none of my events were in this genre of music, but Latin music in Central Florida was on the verge of blowing up. I began putting together an event that would take me nine months to produce. It was a Latin music festival featuring Celia Cruz, Tito Puente, and other Latin groups. The event was called Festival Caribe '93. I wanted to replicate the success of the Calle Ocho festival in Miami, the biggest Latin cultural festival in Florida.

While I was coordinating the logistics and marketing for this festival, I closed a deal with a local club in downtown Orlando to produce a Latin night. I figured this would help me penetrate the Latin scene in Orlando and help to promote my festival. I was offered Wednesday nights at Club Dekkos. I pushed for Thursday nights and got it. For the next nine months, I produced a Latin night at Club Dekkos every Thursday night, which turned out to be one of the best decisions I ever made. It was a great deal. They paid for all of the promotion and advertising. I had complete discretion on where and how the advertising budget would be spent. I paid only for the night's talent or entertainment. They kept 100 percent of the bar revenues, and I kept 100 percent of the admission and ticket sales.

Because I had Thursdays rather than Friday or Saturday nights, I was able to offer touring bands that flew into Florida an off-night for an extra show. What I mean by that is, when bands traveled to Florida to perform, they would typically have only Friday and Saturday night gigs to work. No one else was offering live shows on weekdays. It didn't make sense for the bands to stick around for an entire week until the next weekend to work because the costs of hotel rooms, per diems, and transportation would be prohibitive. But I was offering a Thursday night venue, and booking agents would book their touring artist into my club so they could work three dates in the market instead of just two. It was also cheaper for me because I didn't have to carry the cost of flying everyone into the state. They would bus up from Miami or Tampa. I became the go-to guy for Latin music in Central Florida. I didn't have to pick up the phone to call agents for any artists. Now, they were all calling me. I booked just about everyone who was looking to tour in Central and South Florida.

During this time, Juan Toro, the main booking agent for Ralph Mercado Management (RMM) and the principal agent I dealt with for Latin music, contacted me to see if I would be interested in booking a kid by the name of Marc Anthony. He sent me a promo kit on him, and I took a look at it. This guy did not fit your typical salsa artist image. He had long hair, glasses, and an urban New York edge to him. Juan told me that the cost would be $4,000 plus airfares, hotel, ground transportation, and per diems. I said he was crazy. There was no way I would pay that. So I left his promotional packet sitting on my desk and left it at that.

One day soon after that, a disc jockey from the local AM radio station came into my office to sell me adverting spots for my festival with Celia Cruz and Tito Puente. She had a brokered time slot at the radio station and also owned a small mom-and-pop record store. When she saw the promo kit for Marc Anthony, her eyes opened wide. She was clearly excited about it. She asked me if I was going to bring him down for a show. I said no, and she immediately looked disappointed. I was intrigued enough by that conversation and her reaction that I contacted Juan Toro and told him that I was interested in Marc Anthony but that I was not willing to pay what he was asking for. He told me that I was in luck, because Marc was going to be in Miami for a private event with Juan Gabriel, and I could have him at my club for $1,500 delivered plus two rooms and that Marc would do six songs to track. We closed the deal, and I sold out the date. The event went well, and we really hit it off. For the next year, Juan Toro would ask me if I would be willing to come to New York to work as Marc Anthony's road manager. I said no at the time because I had never been to New York, and I was, quite frankly, afraid to take such a leap.

The following year, around February 1994, I secured an exclusive deal with the UCF arena for Latin music and was producing salsa concerts. In March of that year, I brought Marc Anthony back to perform, this time with his entire band to do their complete show. Once again, for the two weeks leading up to the show at the UCF arena, Juan Toro made offers for me to come up and work with him.

He had just left RMM and was working with David Maldonado Entertainment (DME). David Maldonado was Marc Anthony's manager and had just split up with Ralph Mercado to go on his own. Juan Toro went with David and was looking to build up his team. This time I didn't pass on the offer. Two weeks after the Marc Anthony show, I sold everything I could, loaded everything I had left into my Toyota Tercel, and moved to New York City.

7

THE APPRENTICE

WORKING AT DAVID MALDONADO Entertainment was one of the most enjoyable times in my life. The people there were like a family to me. I grew to love David like a father, and he became someone I wanted to emulate. He was a unique character, and his vast experience and knowledge of the Latin music business was inspiring and awesome to witness. Juan Toro was my personal mentor and close friend. I learned so much from working with him and watching him negotiate with the promoters and with the artists. Juan was a seasoned agent and well respected in the industry. He was in charge of all the major artists on DME's roster. It wasn't much of a roster as they had only Marc Anthony as an exclusively signed artist. However, they had gained respect in the industry as an agency that finds work for the artists, so they worked with just about every artist. I learned quickly that the artists were, as Juan put it, "hoes." They wanted to work, and they would work with whoever could get them a gig. Latin artists seldom signed exclusive deals. Rather, they would let any agent contact them directly and offer them work. So the agency with the most contacts or relationships with talent buyers had the most leverage and appeal.

I was new to this side of the business. For years, I had been the guy on the outside, the one paying for the privilege of having the artist perform. Outside of that, there was no recognition from the artist or the industry. No one cared about the promoters—at least not from where I'd been sitting. But on this side of the fence, it was different. Artists knew who you were. You could sit with them, see what they were working on, and hear what they wanted to do. On this side, I was introduced to record executives, record promoters, radio station executives, program directors, and talent buyers from all around the world. It was a smorgasbord of opportunities and possibilities.

Unlike Juan Toro, however, I didn't have any credibility or experience yet. I was a rookie. So I was relegated to working with the developing acts—up-and-coming hopefuls signed to major and independent labels, one hit wonders, and some that were beginning to significantly penetrate the scene. I worked with them to figure out how to get them work and how to make money for the agency. I served as an agent and as a road manager. I had to be creative, resourceful, and relentless. I did not get paid much. Most of my money came from road managing, because commissions on up-and-coming artists were almost nonexistent. But I was really good at what I did. I took to it like fish to water. I thrived in this space. There was no rock

I didn't look under, no contact I didn't make, no idea too farfetched to pursue. I may have only had the B and C artists on the roster, but that didn't keep me from bringing in half of the company's gross revenues for each of the seven years I worked for DME.

Just to give you an example, I road-managed a merengue group out of Puerto Rico called Grupo Mania. Because they were trying to break into the Northeast, we had to be conservative with the tour expenses. So instead of booking the band in hotels in the city, we booked them into places like a Days Inn in New Jersey just outside of the Holland Tunnel. As I was checking the band into this hotel, I came across a small Spanish newspaper that was on the counter of the front desk. There was an article interviewing a gentleman by the name of José Villa. He was the president of the Hispanic Chamber of Commerce for Hawaii. The article talked about two hundred years of Hispanic heritage in Hawaii and the over two hundred thousand Latinos living there. I was impressed and surprised by what I read.

When I returned to the office, I gave that article to David Maldonado. He read it, shrugged his shoulders and said, "And…?" I said, "David, maybe we should call this guy and see if he wants to bring Marc there for a show." David shrugged his shoulders again and threw the paper into the garbage can. Once again, I felt belittled. Here was a man I had a huge amount of respect for, and he had just shot me down as though I was stupid. I was embarrassed and hurt, but only for a little while.

I took the paper out of the garbage can and called information to get the area code for Hawaii. Then I called information in Hawaii and asked for the Hispanic Chamber of Commerce. They said there is no such listing. I asked for the Chamber of Commerce. They gave me the number, and I called them. (Life without the Internet was a process back then.) When they answered the phone, I said I was trying to reach the president of the Hispanic Chamber of Commerce.

They said, "Oh, you want José Villa." *Bingo!* I got him. They gave me his number, and I called him.

When I finally got hold of José Villa, I explained that I'd learned about him from that article, and that I was impressed with what I'd read. I asked him if he knew who Marc Anthony was. He said no. I told him I would send him a promo kit and follow up with him in a couple of weeks. When he received the promo kit, he was excited. I asked him if he was interested in producing a show in Hawaii for all those Latinos. We discussed price, logistics, expenses, and so on. He did his research and said he could do the show based on the price and terms we'd discussed, but he could not pay for flights out of New York. They were just too expensive. He did say, however, that if he could fly the band out of Los Angeles, he would do it. Great! One problem down and another one to overcome. How do I get Marc Anthony and his band to Los Angeles?

I began contacting every promoter in the United States that DME worked with and asking if they wanted a date with Marc Anthony. They all said, "Who?" You see, at that time Marc had the biggest salsa hit in the country, but he had very little name recognition. He was still a developing artist. I had to sing the song, "*Hasta que Te Conocí*," and remember, I can't sing to save my life. But everyone knew the song was a huge hit, and they were interested. However, none of the promoters felt that Marc had enough marquee name recognition to be able to headline a show on his own. So another problem to solve: How could I get Marc to perform with those promoters without being the headliner?

I learned through Juan Toro that Tony Vega, one of the more established artists Juan worked with, was going to be out on a Northeast tour. So I offered to package a tour with Tony Vega and Marc Anthony. I booked them into Chicago, Houston, San Diego, and Los Angeles. From there, Tony Vega flew back to New York, and

Marc Anthony, the band, and I flew to Hawaii for a gig in the ballroom of the Sheraton Waikiki.

I'd done it. From the garbage can where David had tossed that newspaper, I'd pulled out a multi leg tour and taken a relatively unknown artist to headline in Hawaii. In the process, I also made some money for both DME and me. Interestingly, I managed to do all this within the first six months of working for DME. I started in March 1994, and we performed in Hawaii in August of that same year.

I worked for DME for the next seven years. During that time, I developed a niche for touring developing artists.

8

Bold Moves

As I mentioned, I first moved to New York in March of 1994. I had never been there prior to my move. It was without a doubt a bold step for me. I was amazed at how big the city was and how many people called this place their home. I remember driving west one day on the Belt Parkway in Brooklyn, heading toward Long Island. As I looked toward the right, I noticed a large structure on the horizon, protruding from among the tall buildings just on the edge of the sea. This structure turned out to be the parachute jump at Coney Island at Steeplechase Park. I recall being mesmerized by the buildings on the far south side of the island. As I drove past, I found myself wondering about one in particular, wondering who lived in there. *People have lives here,* I thought. *They go about their daily business; they have family and friends here. Who are these people? What are they like? What do they do?* It was almost overwhelming. I was so new to this big city, and I was realizing just how small I was in the grand scheme of things.

Eight months later, I was on tour with salsa music artist, Edwin Rivera. He had just released his first record out of Puerto Rico and was getting respectable airplay in New York City and other parts of the northeastern United States. He was one of our developing artists, and I was his responsible agent and road manager. I'll never forget the night we were playing a gig at a trendy club called Les Poulets. It had a strong, Wednesday night, after-work crowd, and was known to feature both established and up-and-coming salsa artists.

After we'd set up and the band began to play, I noticed a beautiful woman in the middle of the dance floor. I could not take my eyes off of her. She looked amazing. Her hair was long, black, and wavy. Her eyes were dark with long lashes, and she completely captivated me. She wore a white blouse with a red blazer and a short black skirt. I noticed everything about her. The place was packed full of people, but all I could see was her. I, however, was invisible. Like Charles Dickens' Ghost of Christmas Present, I was looking into a scene where everyone was there but me. She was unaware of my presence or of how deeply I was moved by her.

After the show was over, I was back on the tour bus with the rest of the musicians, counting heads and making sure all the equipment was accounted for. We still had stragglers, and not all of the equipment was loaded onto the bus, so I went back inside to move things along. As I reentered the club, I noticed one of the musicians talking to her—the woman who had captured my attention. I pretended not to notice and continued to walk past, but the musician tapped me on the shoulder and asked me for the contact information for the hotel we were staying in. I pulled out my business card and wrote the information on the back. As I handed it to her, I told her, "My number is on the other side." She looked at me somewhat perplexed, as did the musician. Turns out, she didn't call either one of us.

The following Wednesday, I was back on tour at Les Poulets, but this time with Victor Manuelle. Victor was also getting a significant amount of airplay and was another developing artist I was responsible for. As the band began to play, I noticed the same woman from the week before. This time I wasn't going to let her get away. She was with another woman, who turned out to be someone who occasionally came by our office with another friend—an independent promoter who booked talent from David Maldonado Entertainment for salsa dances and club shows. I didn't know the woman by name, but I recognized her from the office. It turned out she and my mystery woman worked together in the same law firm. *What a coincidence*, I thought. I looked at her and said, "Oh, now you have to go out with me." I gave her my card again and this time asked for her number. The following week we went on our first date.

On the night of our date, we met in the city and went out for dinner and a movie. We had a great time, and then I drove her home. As we got closer to where she lived, I noticed the parachute jump popping out of the night sky as the backdrop to Coney Island. She directed me to take Exit 6 off the Belt Parkway, and we drove down and turned right. I realized that we were heading toward the building that had so mesmerized me a few months back. It wasn't until she told me where to stop that I figured out she lived in that very same building.

Now I knew. I had my answer. I knew who lived there, what she did, what she was like…and it became clear, right then and there, that this was meant to be. What were the odds? Eight million people living in New York City and its five boroughs, and I had found the one person who lived in that specific building and worked with that friend who had another friend who booked talent from the office I work in—all because I took a chance and moved up from Florida. Wow! Saying it today still amazes me.

We continued to date, and I found out she was a single mom. Soon after that, I met her beautiful five-year-old daughter, and it wasn't long before we were a family. Four years later, we got married. We're still together after all these years, with two more lovely daughters. I love my wife, and I thank God for her and my children every day.

9

Working for the Man

ALTHOUGH **I** WORKED FOR DME for seven years, I left twice to go out on my own. I was dissatisfied with the fact that I did not feel appreciated for the work I was doing and the revenues I was producing for the company. I was not just booking talent; I was also creating awareness of DME in the industry. Our tours were becoming increasingly attractive to the artists, their managers, and their record labels.

For example, Victor Manuelle was an up-and-coming recording artist. He was beginning to make some noise, but it was a challenge to book him because he was so new in the industry despite his great talent as a *sonero*—a lead singer who is good at improvising lyrics in salsa music. I was responsible for developing his music at DME. Latin artists generally didn't sign exclusive booking contracts, but David wanted to sign him. I proposed this to Manuelle's management, but they weren't interested. They said they would sign with me but not with DME. I proposed an exclusive contract with DME but with a clause naming me as the key man. This meant that if I left the company, the contract would be voided. They agreed to those terms, and Victor Manuelle signed an exclusive booking deal with DME.

Even though I was responsible for bringing in half of the company's income and had created business opportunities for DME, I was barely making enough money from their salary to get by. In fact, I made more on my side business—a gypsy cab service—than I did at DME. I had two cars and leased each one out for $750 per week. So there I was, bringing in half of DME's yearly revenues and living off of what I was earning on the side. The first time I left DME was in 1995, and it was only for a few months. I left again in 1998, after I married my wife. I was frustrated because I was going nowhere. While I was making money for DME and they were growing their Puerto Rico office and paying their employees well from the revenues I was bringing into the New York office, I had to make my money on the side.

At one point, I went back to school full time for a year at the College of Staten Island, hoping to improve my situation. I had my wife and daughter and one on the way. In order to provide for them, I fell back on my medical training and got a job as a phlebotomist, drawing blood for lab work at the VA in Brooklyn while taking the prerequisite college courses to become a physician's assistant.

Then, in the spring of 1999, I received a call from David Diaz. He had been in the record business for several years and was well known. He was now working as the general manager for DME. He asked if I would be interested in coming back to work on Rubén

Blades' tour. DME wanted me to put together one of my tours, which meant doing what I was best at. The fact that they were calling me to return to DME meant that no one else was able to do it. At least that is how I interpreted it. Now, all those years of making something out of nothing, stringing dates for unknown or developing artists, finding buyers in remote markets, and working way outside the box—they were about to be tested with one of the most iconic artists in the business.

I was very interested in working with Rubén Blades. However, I did not want to go back to the same old cycle of making money for the company while just getting by for myself. So I laid down my terms. I made a deal with DME (and it was agreed to in writing) that (1) I would receive one third of all the commissions I produced and I would get a $500 weekly advance off of that commission, and the balance would be paid to me at the end of the year in one lump sum for all the commissions earned; (2) I would make my own hours; and (3) I didn't have to travel. (I was already burnt out on all the traveling I had done over the last few years.) So that spring, I went back to DME and started to work on Rubén Blades' tour.

I had met Rubén during my previous time at DME, but this was the first time I would work directly with him. I flew to Las Vegas where he was working a private gig with salsa artist Gilberto Santa Rosa. It was the first time I spoke with him and had a chance to discuss the tour. He was releasing his new album, *Tiempos*, on the Sony label, and the tour was designed to market and promote the record. I explained that I would be working on a national ground tour, which was not the norm for Latin artists. Because of the nature of this tour, I would take all offers from buyers across the country and present them all to him. It was not my money, so I was not going to turn down anything. He would have to tell me what he would and would not accept.

I got to work and contacted every talent buyer I could. I worked every possible route, venue, and festival I could find. When it was all ready to be presented, I had organized about thirty days of tour dates and one of the most extensive consecutive tours of Rubén Blades' career. I had offers ranging from $150,000 all the way down to $6,000. Like I said, I did not reject anything. It was not my job to turn down his money, although I knew how ridiculous some of those offers were. I was concerned that Rubén would be pissed off that I would present such low offers to him, two in particular from the same promoter in New Mexico.

Since this was the first time I had worked with Rubén, I did not know how he would react, so I put them in order with the highest offers at the top. The first offer was $150,000 for San Juan, Puerto Rico. The second was $100,000 for the Arthur Ashe Stadium in New York. The two lowest were those New Mexico offers at $8,000 for Albuquerque and $6,000 for Santa Fe. I cannot recall what the amounts were for the offers in between, as they were not particularly remarkable. They were within the range that he usually accepted. What made the top two and the bottom two numbers particularly memorable was Rubén's reaction to them.

When we sat down to go over the dates, he scratched off the Puerto Rico and New York dates and accepted all the rest, including the two New Mexico dates.

I was beside myself. All the artists I had worked with over the years were all about the money. Not Rubén Blades. He had a way of looking at the dates and the offers and judging them, not on the basis of how much he would make but rather what the date meant to him. He was not motivated by the almighty dollar but rather by principle and genuine conviction. I was impressed and became an instant fan of Rubén Blades, the person, not just Rubén Blades, the artist. He had earned my respect.

I later asked him why he'd turned down $250,000 in offers but accepted the two dates in New Mexico. He told me that he did not want to go back to Puerto Rico just yet, and that since he was returning from an extensive European tour the day prior to the New York date, he wanted his band to rest. I thought, what an amazing guy. All those years of working with artists who were all about themselves privately while portraying something else publicly, and here was a guy who actually walked the walk. He said he wanted to do New Mexico because he had never performed there and he wanted to go back to where he'd filmed the Robert Redford movie, *The Milagro Bean Field War*.

Later that year we went out on the tour. I say "we" because, despite my deal that I did not have to travel, I wanted to make sure everything went well with Rubén's tour. I was impressed with the man and wanted to know more about him, so we went out and traveled across the country. I did not go to all the dates, but I went to many of them. I went on interviews with him and got to know him more and more. To say that I had the utmost respect for Rubén is an understatement. He was insightful, highly intellectual, and surprisingly simple. He did not want first-class flights, hotel suites, or limousines. He liked talking with people and was gracious to everyone who approached him. He loved to tell stories, and everyone around him enjoyed hearing them. The tour was a success, and Rubén was nominated for and won a Grammy for *Tiempos*.

Then, at the end of 1999, it came time to settle up with DME for the remaining balance of my commissions. I sat down with Juan Toro, who explained to me that they just didn't have it and would have to renegotiate the amount. I was pissed off. I was owed $37,000, and all they offered me was $7,000. I gave them a thirty-day notice and told them I was resigning at the end of the year. To be honest, I didn't want to leave. I really didn't care about the money; it was a matter of principle. I had already tried it on my own twice before and knew it was not going to be easy. I had two daughters now, one just six months old, and a wife to think about. Life was no longer just about me. I had responsibilities. I gave DME thirty days because I wanted to give them plenty of time to ask me to stay. I thought that if they realized what I was producing for them, they would see my worth and work something out with me.

In the meantime, I went ahead with my plan to go on my own. I asked Arturo Martinez if he wanted to come with me, telling him that I would make him a partner. Arturo was a good junior agent at DME. He didn't particularly book many dates, but he worked well with people and was street smart. He could figure things out and had a great temperament to deal with some of the artists' prima donna attitudes that I had absolutely no tolerance for. He said he would, and we flipped a coin and decided on a name for the company. When I told Rubén that we were going on our own, he said if we opened our own agency, he would come with us. I was surprised. I really was not expecting that and neither was Arturo.

Then, sure enough, when the time came for me to leave DME, David Maldonado himself called me into his office. He said to me in the most endearing manner possible, "Come on, kid. Why do you want to leave?" He was a character all right, and that's what I loved about him. I remember watching him get on the phone and curse out Ralph Mercado, yelling at the top of his voice, "Fuck you, you motherfucker!" Then fifteen minutes later, he'd call him up for a deal as if nothing had ever happened. You couldn't hate David, even when he was cursing you out.

So when he called me into his office, I said, "David, I don't want to leave, but you leave me no choice. If you want me to stay, give me something—anything!—so that I don't feel like a jerk for staying. Give me 1 percent partnership; I don't care, crumbs, just something."

He said no, and I said that I was going on my own. Then he went from good cop to bad cop. He said I wouldn't last three months, that it was a dog-eat-dog business, and I would be destroyed, that I didn't stand a chance. I told him that if I failed, I would do it on my own terms, and with that, I terminated my employment with DME for the third and final time.

10

ROLLING THE DICE

So there I was. It was January 1, 2000. We survived the Y2K end-of-times apocalypse, and I was on my own with a new company, Martinez, Morgalo & Associates. I was working out of our tiny two-bedroom apartment in Brooklyn. I had no money and no prospects for the time being. I had to think fast if I was going to make it.

About this time, a young up-and-coming salsa artist by the name of Luis Damon was making some noise on the charts and in the clubs. I spoke with the label and told them that if they subsidized Damon's tour, I could book more than thirty gigs across the United States. That was a very bold statement and a huge gamble. But I knew I had no choice. If they gave me the money, I would have to deliver the dates.

I showed them a list of dates, cities, and venues where I would book the artist, but they were just letters and numbers on a paper. None of those dates were confirmed. They agreed to give me $10,000. That was enough to get me started. My desk was a glass dining table in the cramped living room of my apartment. I had a map of the United States on the wall in front of the table and my phone by my side. I started calling every promoter, every mom-and-pop record store, every Latin food restaurant, radio station, and DJ I could find. I pushed and pushed until I got every single date I'd promised. It was something to see. Nonstop calls and follow-ups and mailings and singing on the phone. (Did I mention I can't sing worth a crap?) Sometimes I wondered if they booked the date just so I would stop singing. I might not have been able to sing, but it sure did feel like I was making a living out of it. And if it worked, I didn't care what I sounded like.

It took me a couple of months to close all those deals. I put together a tour that had never been done before with a Latin salsa artist. There were thirty-two confirmed shows in thirty-six days, all by bus with a fifteen-piece orchestra. There were just four days off in the entire tour—all back-to-back dates. This was by far the most ambitious thing I had ever done. This was such a big deal that I was featured on the cover of *Billboard* magazine on the July 22, 2000, edition under the title, "Innovative Route for Latino Tours," with an article by Ray Waddell. Imagine that, six months in business and already making the cover of *Billboard*.

By March 2000, Arturo Martinez was finally on board full time. It took him a while to make the final jump. He was unsure, and I didn't blame him. He was married and had kids too. Making a move like that without any guarantees is not something to take lightly. But, with our operations finally in place, we started booking artists. We booked Rubén Blades, Luis Damon, Son by Four, Oscar D'León, El Gran Combo de Puerto Rico, Willie Colón, Flaco Jiménez, Luis Enrique, Patrick Shannon, and many more. What made us particularly successful was that we didn't only consider our artists as our clients; we also considered our talent buyers as our clients. Our main priority was to aggressively find work for our artists. However, on the flip side of that, we also worked aggressively to help our talent buyers find talent, whether we represented them or not. To our artists we worked as agents; to our talent buyers, we worked as talent buyers. We helped them fill open dates and last-minute cancellations.

I stayed home most of the time while Arturo traveled with the artists. Sometimes I would travel with Rubén Blades, but very seldom did I find myself having to leave my family. By August 2000, I was doing well enough that I could buy our first home. It's hard to believe—seven years working for DME and I had barely been able to pay my bills; yet in less than eight months out on my own, I was able to purchase a house.

I didn't want my daughters to grow up in the city, so we bought a house in Pennsylvania. It was both a sacrifice and a blessing. My wife and kids had a wonderful home in a quiet and safe neighborhood, but I had to drive more than two hours each way every day. I didn't complain. I wasn't traveling on the road and was home every night to kiss my children and my wife. Those long hours of driving were actually an unintentional blessing of commuting back and forth between New York and Pennsylvania. I didn't listen to the radio during the drive in either direction. This was my sanctuary, my "me" time. I had plenty of time to think and develop strategies.

On one particular night in early 2001, I was trying to think of somewhere in New York City that I could book Rubén Blades where he had not already played. I wanted to find something interesting, something that would be good publicity for him and his career. He had already played Madison Square Garden, the Beacon Theatre, Carnegie Hall, Lehman College, and the Brooklyn Academy of Music, to name a few. I didn't want him to do just another show. As I drove home from my office, I pictured the subway map in my head and started to pan down from the Bronx. When I got to Harlem, I thought about the Apollo Theater. My heart began to race. I could feel it pounding in my chest. *The Apollo Theater*, I thought. *No one has ever done a Latin concert there!* If Rubén played the Apollo, it would be newsworthy.

I knew I was onto something, but I could not do the show alone as it would have been a conflict of interest, since I represented Rubén. I also knew I couldn't call David Maldonado, Henry Cardenas, or Ralph Mercado. Each of them were successful promoters who were astute in the business. One wrong move on my part, and they could take the idea and run with it.

I decided to contact Larry Stein from Rocktropic Productions, a promoter out of Puerto Rico. He was always trying to get a date with Rubén—in fact, he was the promoter who'd made the offer for Puerto Rico that Rubén had turned down on our first tour together in 1999. I called him immediately, while I was still on my way home—and no, I didn't have to sing this time. This time the stars were in alignment, and Rubén was no developing artist. Larry wasn't sure if it would work at first, but I explained that doing this event at the Apollo would be newsworthy and a milestone in Latin music history. He was in.

The next day I called the Apollo Theater. I spoke with Charlie Sutton, who was in charge of booking the theater. She was excited to have Rubén Blades perform at the Apollo. So the deal was coming together. Next I called Rubén and asked him if he was interested in playing the Apollo. There was no hesitation. He said yes right away.

I knew that I was on to something here. I needed to secure an exclusivity contract with the Apollo so no one could undermine what I was doing. I tried to get the Apollo Theater Foundation to give me an exclusive deal for Latin music; however, they would not do that. So I asked if they could at least guarantee that no other Latin music event would take place thirty days prior or thirty days after my events. They agreed to that and put it in writing. So I booked ten concerts as part of a series and spread them out over several months in the year. I had my exclusivity, and no one else could book another Latin show while I was there. Rubén Blades sold out two back-to-back shows at the Apollo in June 2001, and once again I was featured in *Billboard* magazine. Things were looking up.

Then came 9/11.

11

THEN EVERYTHING CHANGED

SEPTEMBER 11, 2001, STARTED out just like any other day. I left my home in Pennsylvania and headed to New York City on my morning commute to the office. As usual, I stopped at the halfway point, a 7-Eleven near the Lehigh Valley area. While I was gassing up my car, Arturo called. He told me that a plane had crashed into the World Trade Center. My first thought was that it was a small plane and that traffic would be a mess in the Holland Tunnel. I began to tell him that I was just going to work out of the house, and then I heard him say, "Oh shit! Another plane hit the other tower!"

I knew instantly that it was no coincidence. I told him I had to get my family and hung up. I called my wife at work and told her to go pick up our youngest daughter from daycare, and I would pick up our oldest. Then on the radio, I heard about the plane that hit the Pentagon. From that moment forward, things would never be the same. Everything changed.

As the days progressed, I was moved by the stories on the news of families who'd lost their wives, husbands, children, parents, and by all those who stepped up to help—the firefighters, police, military, and civilians alike. There was no division in our country. No cracks in our solidarity. These attacks brought everyone together. I felt I needed to do something, but I didn't know what. I was a medic in the Army Reserves, but I had been in the IRR (Individual Ready Reserve) for several years at that time. The IRR is a component of the US Army Reserves, but one that does not require members to report to monthly battle assemblies. It is merely a database of soldiers who are available in the event of a national emergency. I called Human Resources Command (HRC) and told them I wanted to help. They transferred me from the IRR to an army reserve unit in Bethlehem, Pennsylvania, the 744th Military Police Battalion. My first battle assembly was in November 2001.

I was back on active reserve status, but I continued to run and operate my business. I participated in battle assemblies one weekend per month and annual training for two weeks per year. Nationally, things were getting back to normal, but our company was still in recovery mode.

The top three industries most affected by the attacks were the financial, travel, and entertainment industries. That last quarter of 2001 almost closed down Martinez, Morgalo & Associates. Existing tours were cancelled, future tours were on hold, promoters didn't want to risk any further losses, and we were struggling to fill our seats at the Apollo. I had to take action to ensure we continued our operations.

Larry Stein didn't want to continue with the Apollo series, but I didn't want to quit. So I negotiated a deal with him to retain the exclusive rights to the Latin Nites at the Apollo concert series. I called a meeting with our sponsor, Chivas Regal. They had paid $100,000 in sponsorship for ten shows, and we had produced only five. At that meeting, I explained to their executives that I could continue with the series even though there was no turn out and fulfill my legal obligation, but that having empty seats would not serve them well. I proposed to postpone the events until 2002 and start all over with another ten shows. I offered to give them a $50,000 credit toward the next year's sponsorship. They were grateful for my candor and agreed to my terms. The following year I charged them $250,000 in sponsorship and received $200,000 in January of 2002. In addition to this, I applied for and received an SBA disaster relief loan for $50,000, which was also paid to us in the first quarter of 2002.

That year was a particularly good year for the company. Judging from the testimony at trial from my former partner, however, you would think we were in financial distress. But the fact remains that we received in excess of $750,000 to subsidize our entire operations, which now focused mostly on the Apollo concert series and less on booking talent. In fact, our total commission from Rubén Blades that year was $100,000. That is $100,000 for our operations—payroll for ten people, office rent, office supplies, travel, etc.—for a whole year. Compare that to the $750,000. The argument made at trial, which you will see later, was that the shows at the Apollo were not going well and weren't selling tickets.

However, even if every show had not sold a single ticket—even if we had given away every ticket for every single show—we still would have made a profit. You see, spread out over ten shows, the sponsorships amounted to $75,000 per show. Our average budget per show was $60,000. This means that, even if we had given away every ticket, we would still have made about $15,000 per show. But we *did* sell tickets, and the concert series *was* lucrative for the company. It's what sustained us and paid our employees and our overhead. And, yes, we had debt. We had creditors that needed to be paid and monies owed. But that was all part of managing a business. We aged our accounts payables while expediting our accounts receivables. We leveraged our assets and expanded our business. We worked off of our cash flow and kept the doors open. We valued the artists we represented and the promoters we dealt with.

12

MIXING IT UP

NOW THAT YOU HAVE a good understanding about my business and my life, I think it's important to also understand the dispute between Willie Colón and Rubén Blades and how it got started.

The news that Willie Colón was suing Rubén Blades came as a huge shock to those who followed their careers and to the Latin music community in general. These were two of the biggest names in salsa music history; they had been forever cast by the public as a musical duo, despite the fact that each had been going solo for decades. The shock can largely be attributed to the fact that the discord and animosity between them had remained relatively unknown to the public. There had always been wide speculation and heated debates as to why the two had split up or who was at fault or which of the two was better for the other's career, but the true level of their artistic and personal divide had remained mostly concealed from the public until the news of the lawsuit.

The public impression was that they were great friends and got along well. But privately, it was the total opposite. Behind the scenes, Rubén referred to Willie as the *sombra*—a shadow or dark cloud. He frequently complained that Willie was trying to ride his coattails; yet publicly he praised the opportunity that Willie had given him, helping him start his career by allowing Rubén to join his band. The two had collaborated on many records and toured extensively throughout the world. However, things began to get strained when Willie realized that Rubén was coming to his house for sheet music but was using the music to get gigs without Willie. When the group split up, both Willie and Rubén continued to be successful in their careers, but were seldom seen again on the same stage.

From my perspective, I can say that Rubén Blades demonstrated no interest in any such opportunities to perform with Willie Colón. In fact, he was very clear with Arturo and me that he did not want to be in any show in which Willie was also performing. And not just to perform with each other—he also did not even want to be on the same stage or in the same show on the same night. This was a clear and direct instruction given by Rubén. We received many requests for Rubén and Willie to perform together, but Rubén always turned them down. He always publicly praised Willie for the opportunity he had given him when starting out, but privately he minced no words. I remember Rubén getting very upset once, when a promoter added Willie Colón as a last-minute artist at a Madison Square Garden show where he was going to perform. He thought that it was all a scheme to get them to perform together.

Rubén's distrust and cynicism was constant—always present but not always seen. Every time there was a festival, concert, or any other event that even remotely had a potential for them performing together, the reaction was the same. In spite of this, however, sometimes Rubén would surprise everyone and do something completely out of the ordinary. For example, when Willie Colón was running for public office in New York, Rubén performed at a fundraiser for him. It was always hard to figure him out. It was as if there were an inner struggle brewing—a tug-of-war between his love and admiration for Willie and his complete disdain for him.

From Willie Colón's perspective, all I have to go on are his statements—both public and in his deposition—as well as his own actions. I have never witnessed Willie making any public or private statements that were negative in nature about Rubén. Nor have I ever witnessed any actions that would remotely appear as though he were actively avoiding Rubén. In fact, I observed quite the opposite. Although my dealings with Willie have been significantly more limited than those with Rubén, I have seen enough to discern a true contrast between them. Willie has always demonstrated a willingness—and to some degree, perhaps, even an eagerness—to work with Rubén. Not so with Rubén.

Looking at this from my perspective, then, it was difficult to see how these two men could even consider working together. But in reviewing their depositions, it becomes clearer. Rubén and Willie come from very different backgrounds. As Willie described it, "You know, I come from very, very poor background, and Rubén was more a middle-class kid…taking a break from college…being a tourist in my ghetto."[1]

Willie described Rubén as being "very explosive" at times and "at the drop of a hat, he would start screaming at people hysterically."[2] Willie attributed this as one of the underlying causes of their breakup. He noted, "that was one thing that, with my background, just was not a healthy thing for him to do. So that was one of the real dangers of our thing. You know, that this thing was going to get physical because Rubén is very…he gets very irritable around mortal men."[3]

I can attest to this irritability and volatility. I had witnessed it many times, and I had no tolerance for it. Arturo was better suited to deal with Rubén's temperament. For example, I received a call from a promoter in Chicago who told me that Rubén had just exploded out of nowhere and was yelling and screaming at him in the lobby of the hotel. At first I thought he was joking, so I asked him to put Rubén on the phone. Sure enough, Rubén was out of control, yelling at me and creating an obvious scene in the hotel lobby. His grievance was that the promoter was only paying $15,000 for the show at the House of Blues, but he also had sponsors. This was not like the man I'd first met in 1999, taking a show for $6,000. Nor was it a typical action of a man of his stature. It wasn't like he didn't know in advance what he was getting paid. We did not accept any date that he hadn't approved in advance. I still don't know what got into him on that day, but he was upset that the promoter was "making a killing" off of him.

One of the most fascinating discoveries made about the relationship between these two men, as recalled by Willie Colón, was how he felt Rubén had used him as a means to advance his career. "Right after the first album came out…he called my wife and told her he was coming over for the music. Now, this is when he's my singer. He was coming over for the music, and my wife said, 'Rubén's coming for the music,' and I said, 'For what?' So when I asked him, he said, 'No, I'm going to copy the music.' You know, I just gave the guy a friggin' break, and he's going to copy the music…. So, what he did was, he took my band…and I said, what about me? And he said 'there's not enough money for you.'[4] I'm looking at long-term plans, and I realized that…I was just a stepping stone for him."[5]

It is evident that their musical relationship was very much like a bad marriage. Sure, they had their good times. But the bad just outweighed the good. Their music is like a child in shared custody. Both are responsible for it and have been similarly forced to deal with each other due to its creation and development.

The lawsuit between the two provided the first real glimpse into the relationship of these two artists and the underlying causes that ultimately led to their decisions to separate and, to a certain degree, avoid each other as much as possible. While the public demand for them to reunite perpetually grew, the likelihood of it proportionally diminished.

13

FOLLOW THE BOUNCING BALL

NOW, LET'S GET INTO the context of the legal battle that ensued between the parties. The legal case is pretty simple and straightforward. Three claims were filed. One was by Willie Colón against Rubén Blades for breach of contract; the second was by me against Rubén Blades and Rubén Blades Productions, Inc. for defamation; and the third was a cross claim by Rubén Blades against Robert Morgalo (me) and Martinez, Morgalo & Associates. However, there are some matters that if not properly predicated could cloud the issues and make the discussion difficult to follow. So keep your eyes on the bouncing ball. In this case, the bouncing ball is a $62,500 cash deposit.

This amount will come up many times during the rest of this book, as it has throughout the depositions, testimonies, trial transcripts, and documents entered into evidence in this case. This amount represents a deposit paid, in fact, in advance for a Rubén Blades concert in 2002. The event was subsequently cancelled. However, there is much disagreement as to whether that deposit was forfeited due to the promoter's cancellation of the Rubén Blades concert or if it was to be applied to the *Siembra* concert in 2003 with Willie Colón and Rubén Blades. This $62,500 is at the heart of the alleged "missing monies" from that now infamous *Siembra* reunion concert.

The promoter's representative for this initial $62,500 was Ariel Rivas, on behalf of a company called Rompeolas Productions. You will see through the testimonies of the parties and the supporting documents in this book, that Ariel Rivas had no relationship with Rubén Blades prior to the *Siembra* concert. However, Rivas ended up working with Rubén Blades following the *Siembra* concert as one of his representatives, and he also became one of three witnesses Rubén Blades used at trial in his defense against the defamation lawsuit. You will also see the contract for that initial Rubén Blades concert in 2002 involving the deposit of $62,500, which states very clearly that any cancellation by the promoter would result in forfeit of the deposit (see Appendix A). That deposit of $62,500 was paid to Martinez, Morgalo & Associates through a series of wire transfers specifically for a Rubén Blades show from the bank account of César Sáinz for Rompeolas Productions (see Appendix B, minus a receipt for $12,500, which was paid May 21, 2002, as confirmed at the default hearing[1]).

Finally, you will see that there is absolutely no documentation at all authorizing that initial deposit to be used or applied toward the *Siembra* concert. In fact, based on everyone's testimony in the case, the only one making that assertion was Ariel Rivas, who was also the only person who would benefit from such a claim. I have adamantly denied that I agreed to any such allocation of those funds and have maintained that the initial deposit was forfeited. I have also presented evidence showing that wire transfers totaling $50,000 were, in fact, paid to Rubén Blades Productions on December 10, 2002. These transfers represented the payment for that cancelled show, minus the $12,500 commission that was earned by Martinez, Morgalo & Associates, Inc. (see Appendix C).

The importance of the information I just discussed is that there were two events, two contracts completely separate from each other. The first was a show with Rubén Blades in Puerto Rico for an amount of $125,000 that was to take place in December 2002, of which a $62,500 deposit was paid. This amount represented 50 percent of the total artist fees due to Rubén Blades, which were forfeited by the promoter because the show was cancelled. The second contract was for the *Siembra* concert with Willie Colón and Rubén Blades in Puerto Rico. The *Siembra* contract was for an amount of $350,000, and that contract was with Ariel Rivas and a company called Dissar Productions (not Rompeolas, which was the promoter for the Rubén Blades December concert). As it turns out, there were three different versions of that *Siembra* contract, all of which were dated January 22, 2003—after I was deployed—and to this date, no one has been able to produce a single signed contract.

Of the three versions of the *Siembra* contract, the first version states that a deposit of $62,500 was to be paid immediately; the promoter listed was Ariel Rivas of Dissar Productions; and the agent was Arturo Martinez for Martinez, Morgalo & Associates, for the services of (f/s/o) Rubén Blades and Willie Colón (see Appendix D). The second version states that a deposit of $62,500 was received in April 2002 (almost a year earlier—the *Siembra* concert idea wasn't even conceived at that point), the promoter was shown to be Ariel

Rivas of Dissar Productions, and the agent was Arturo Martinez for Martinez, Morgalo & Associates, for the services of (f/s/o) Rubén Blades and Willie Colón (see Appendix E). The third version also states that a deposit of $62,500 was received in April 2002, but the promoters in this version of the contract are listed as César Sáinz of Rompeolas, and Ariel Rivas of Dissar Records, and the agent still listed as Arturo Martinez for Martinez, Morgalo & Associates, Inc., for the services of (f/s/o) Rubén Blades (see Appendix F). Note that Willie Colón's name is not shown on this one, and César Sáinz is suddenly added to the contract. Furthermore, I have to make note of the fact that my name does not appear on any of the three versions of the *Siembra* contract.

Now that we have established the foundations of the controversies, I will present some information that establishes when the *Siembra* concert was confirmed and by whom. For the purpose of maintaining a reference point of when I was still with the company and when I was not with the company due to my deployment, we will set the date of January 16, 2003. So there are events that occurred predeployment and events that occurred postdeployment. January 16, 2003, is the chronological line of meridian that you will reference so that you can be clear as to where I was at any given point throughout this story.

On January 20, 2003, Arturo Martinez sent an e-mail to Willie Colón asking him if the date of May 3, 2003, was available for him to participate in the *Siembra* concert and whether he could confirm that date (see Appendix G). On January 21, 2003, Ariel Rivas sent a proposal letter to Arturo Martinez for the *Siembra* show (see Appendix H). Then on January 22, 2003, Arturo Martinez wrote a letter to César Sáinz and Ariel Rivas, confirming the exclusive appearance of Rubén Blades and Willie Colón for a show at the Hiram Bithorn Stadium to be held on May 3, 2003 (see Appendix I). On that same date, January 22, 2003, the three versions of the *Siembra* contract were drafted.

Once again, I want to remind you that when these e-mails, confirmations, and contracts were written, I was no longer working with the company due to being called to active duty. The supporting documents, which were presented as evidence in both the *Willie Colón v. Rubén Blades* case and the *Robert Morgalo v. Rubén Blades* case and cross claim, clearly establish when the *Siembra* show was confirmed and by whom. The record is clear that my name was not mentioned in any of these documents.

14

THE MAN IN THE MIDDLE

ITHINK IT'S TIME YOU get to know Ariel Rivas a little better. He is, after all, a main supporting cast member in this drama and the one person who insists I authorized him to apply the now famous $62,500 to the *Siembra* show. His testimony is crucial to this case. He was a party to all the relevant contract negotiations. He was the producer of the *Siembra* show and was one of Rubén Blades' star witnesses. Additionally, he is now one of Rubén Blades' representatives.

I first met Ariel sometime in early to midsummer of 2001. It was the first year of the Latin Nites at the Apollo concert series, just before the attacks of 9/11. He was the artist representative for

Danny Rivera, whom we booked for two concerts at the Apollo The-ater. However, per Ariel's testimony and a letter he wrote that was submitted into evidence, Ariel first met my partner, Arturo Marti-nez, some time earlier in 2001, at an event with Rubén Blades and Paul Simon in Los Angeles for the Grammys.[1] Ariel was trying un-successfully to get a show date with Rubén for Puerto Rico. But it wasn't until the night of the concert at the Apollo that I actually met Ariel Rivas. It was also there that Ariel became aware that I repre-sented Rubén Blades.

He contacted me after the Danny Rivera shows and presented several offers to me. The first was for a concert in Santo Domingo with Rubén Blades and Danny Rivera. Although I took him serious-ly, he did not present himself to be very reliable. While I was waiting on his offer for Santo Domingo, I received another offer through Juan Toro's office for Santo Domingo. I could not reach Ariel for some time, so I presented the Santo Domingo date from Juan Toro to Rubén, and he accepted it. That show took place in early 2002. When Ariel finally showed up, he was upset to lose the date but accepted his responsibility in losing it. He explained and testified later in court that he had gone to Cuba for a Danny Rivera concert and had no means of communicating with me. He then submitted another offer, this time for Rubén Blades to perform with Cheo Fe-liciano in Puerto Rico in December 2002. (This is the Rubén Blades concert that was cancelled, for which the promoter forfeited the $62,500.)

The offer was for $125,000 for Rubén Blades to perform. Ariel had to deal with Cheo Feliciano separately, as I did not represent him. Rubén accepted the offer, and we entered into a contract. That contract was drafted on May 30, 2002. The promoter or purchaser is listed as "César Sáinz for Rompeolas," which was the company that was producing the show, and I was listed as the agent. According to the contract, a deposit of $62,500 was to be paid "no later than June 7, 2002" (see Appendix A). However, the full deposit was not paid when it was due.

Instead, I received several delays and excuses from Ariel and assurances that he would send the money. When we finally started to get the deposits, they were paid in smaller amounts over a period of time. In fact, we received the $62,500 in wire transfers as follows: $12,500 (representing 10 percent of the total artist fees and our company's commissions) was paid on May 21, 2002;[2] a second deposit in the amount of $20,000 on June 27, 2002; a third deposit in the amount of $20,000 on October 3, 2002; and a fourth deposit in the amount of $10,000 was sent on October 29, 2002. That completed the total deposit of $62,500 (see Appendix B). As you can see, the deposits were not paid as agreed to by the terms of the contract (see Appendix A).

It is important to note that each of the aforementioned wire transfers for the December show deposits clearly stated that the money was for the Rubén Blades show in Puerto Rico (not the *Siembra* show) and did not include Willie Colón. Also, all of these payments showed César Sáinz/Rompeolas making the payments, not Ariel Rivas or Dissar Productions. This is important because later you will see that, first, the *Siembra* show contracts and deposits do not add up to the contracted amount; second, they were not paid as agreed to the terms of the contract; third, the payments came from Ariel Rivas of Dissar Productions (not César Sáinz of Rompeolas); and finally, the wire transfers from Ariel Rivas made it clear that they were for the *Siembra* show, not the December show.

Approximately one month before the Rubén Blades show was to take place in Puerto Rico, Ariel Rivas contacted me to explain that another salsa show was booked in the same venue on the same weekend as the Rubén Blades show. This show was with Richie Ray and Bobby Cruz, and it was in the same genre as the Rubén Blades and Cheo Feliciano show. Ariel explained that he would stand to lose a lot of money, and he asked if he could postpone the show. I said no. I made it clear that I had kept Rubén out of the Puerto Rico market for almost the entire year of 2002 in order to make this a more exclusive date for him. I also explained to Ariel that we don't assume the risks with the promoter. If he made a million dollars in profit, we could not demand a penny more in artist fees. Likewise, if he lost money on the show, he could not demand a discount on the artist fees. He knew the risks, and neither Rubén nor I were his partners. Also, he should have been aware of the situation much sooner. He contracted with me for that December show in May. If he had secured the venue when we entered into that contract, then the promoters for the Richie Ray and Bobby Cruz show would not have booked on the same weekend, and he would not have had to move, postpone, or cancel his show.

Ariel was not happy about this. He tried everything he could to convince me to move the date. I said no. I was curious as to why he was so anxious about the deposit. He was a promoter with experience, and the contract clearly stated that any cancellation would result in a forfeiture of deposits. I can only assume he had other commitments that put him in a position where he could not afford to lose that money. I didn't know what his dealings were with those other obligations, but to be honest, they were none of my concern. My responsibility was to Rubén Blades. So on December 10, 2002, I wire-transferred a total of $50,000 to Rubén Blades Productions (see Appendix C). This represented the artist fees for Rubén Blades from the $62,500 minus the $12,500 commission that was earned by Martinez, Morgalo & Associates.

Then on January 18, 2003, two days after I received my call to report to active duty, my wife threw a surprise going-away party for me. When I arrived home that day from my military reserve unit, I was definitely surprised. But I was even more surprised to see Ariel Rivas there. He came to my house with Arturo. Apparently he'd flown from Puerto Rico to New York and Arturo drove him to my house in Pennsylvania.

My wife had invited close friends, family members, and members of our church family, including the pastor. It was a very emotional time for me. Writing this all down brings back emotions I have not felt in a long time. I remember how it hit me: the reality that I was going to war, that I would not see my wife and children for who knows how long or if ever again. Then, in the middle of all this, Ariel asks to speak with me. Again, he tried to negotiate something with Rubén. I told him I was with my family, getting ready to deploy. I felt his request was inappropriate. I told him he would need to talk to Arturo from that point on. I had other things to worry about.

Perhaps this is where the misunderstanding began. Could Ariel have misinterpreted my telling him to talk to Arturo from that point on as an indication for him to apply those funds to a later date? I made it clear that he'd lost the funds; I made it clear that I was going away and my mind was somewhere else. However, could it be possible that in his desperation he believed that my telling him to talk to Arturo was an authorization to move forward with his plans? In that moment, I didn't have time to deal with it. Three days later I deployed.

On January 20, 2003, at 7:00 p.m., Arturo sent an e-mail to Willie Colón. In that e-mail he wrote, "Hi Willie, I hope upon receipt of this message all is well.... Below is a list of songs Rubén checked off. I know you sent me five songs you already have, but can you check off which of the following songs you have arrangements for? On another note, I was explaining to Mrs. Colón that most of the venues are requesting dates in July/August (gives us more time to prepare) due to the magnitude of the show and larger venues. The one show we have pending is for Puerto Rico on the 3rd of May. Mrs. Colón said the date seemed OK. We are about to lock in the show (I have to get an estimate of the expenses *all-inclusive show*) and I just wanted to confirm the date was open" (see Appendix G).

According to this communication from Arturo to Willie Colón, it is clear that the *Siembra* date was not yet confirmed as of January 20, 2003. Also, it is clear that Arturo was referencing other shows for July and August and that Rubén had "checked off" on the songs. So they were working on it. Then, on January 21, 2003, Ariel Rivas sent a letter to Arturo Martinez, requesting, among many things, that the promotion for the *Siembra* show would begin in February 2003, and that the artist fee or "cache" be $300,000 (see Appendix I). As you will soon see, both of these terms are important. This letter also referenced the $62,500 as already being paid. The letter stated, "We have complied with the corresponding deposits to Rubén Blades' show, punctually and whenever you requested it of us. The case being that you already have the first $62,500 that we sent some months ago."

Ariel claims at this time that he'd paid the deposits to Rubén Blades' show totaling $62,500 "punctually." However, the wire-transfer dates show otherwise as stated earlier (see Appendix B). Furthermore, except for the three versions of the *Siembra* contract, this is the first time that the $62,500 from Rubén's December show was tied to the *Siembra* show.

From this point on, Ariel claimed and has maintained that I authorized that allocation of funds, which I have always denied. We met once, and he made an offer for Rubén to play Santo Domingo. He didn't follow through on that date, and I booked it with another promoter. Then he made another offer for Rubén, this time in Puerto Rico. He did not make the payments for those deposits as agreed to and then cancelled the show just a month before the event. He clearly was not demonstrating credibility with me.

On top of that, this guy was not my friend. He was not my confidant. We didn't go fishing together. He didn't know my wife's name or my kids' names. He was someone with whom I did business—or at least someone I *tried* to do business with. To tell the truth, nothing he proposed to me actually materialized into a show. But he claims that I am such a good guy that I would let him apply Rubén's money toward another show and that I would forgo my own commissions and work for free. That is exactly what it would mean. We had already earned the $12,500 commission on his cancelled Rubén Blades show, and I had already sent Rubén his money. But Ariel Rivas insists that I authorized that transfer.

Now take a look at the February date that Ariel referenced in the letter to start the promotion of the *Siembra* show. He wrote specifically, "It is extremely important to us to begin the promotion at least three months in advance or better yet, as of next February" (see Appendix I). Remember this letter was written on January 21, 2003. The contract for the *Siembra* show was not yet confirmed; none of the contract versions had even been drafted yet. What makes this date important is that when Ariel Rivas testified at the default hearing, he was asked why he did not make the *Siembra* payments as stipulated on the *Siembra* contracts. He responded that because tickets for the *Siembra* show were selling poorly, it was agreed that they would pay as the tickets sold. When asked with whom he made that arrangement, he said, "with Robert Morgalo." When asked when he'd made those arrangements he said, "Sometime in November, December, January."[3] No one caught that. Not my attorneys, not Willie Colón's attorney, and I am assuming not Rubén Blades' attorney, either. How could I have agreed to those payment arrangements on those dates when the contract was not confirmed until January

2003? And how could the ticket sales be slow if they were not going to go on sale until February 2003?

More importantly, in his letter to Rubén Blades dated May 10, 2003, Ariel Rivas wrote, "We always made the deposits the way *Arturo* authorized us" (emphasis mine).[4] This concurs with what Arturo testified at the default hearing when he was asked by Rubén's attorney, "Specifically for the *Siembra* show, who sent the intervals?" Arturo said, "I believe I did, as far as the intervals."[5]

The main question is, how could a deposit for a contract that was not drafted or confirmed until January 22, 2003, be received in April 2002? How could a $62,500 deposit be paid almost a year before that contract was even created? Yet, that is what the *Siembra* contract states. All three contract versions were written by Arturo Martinez. This is all based on the testimonies of the parties and the evidence presented during discovery.

15

Battle on Two Fronts

O NCE THE *SIEMBRA* CONTRACT was established by those involved, the next few months went on as usual, based on what has been discussed in testimony, documents, and what I have been able to uncover through the discovery process of the case. I was not around for any of it. This was during the first wave of the offensive in Iraq in early 2003. I first arrived in Kuwait on March 11[1] with my unit, and shortly thereafter we crossed the border into Iraq. We had no electricity, no running water, no bathrooms, and no communication with the outside world. We were in a combat zone. I had no time to think about the affairs of my business. All of my thoughts, energy, and focus were on the mission at hand, the welfare of my fellow soldiers, and staying alive. When I did have time for reflection and thoughts of home, they surely were not on the state of my business. Rather, they were on my wife and children. I had no way to contact them, and they had no way of contacting me.

After we crossed the Kuwait/Iraq border, we set up headquarters in Tallil Air Base in An Nasiriyah, Iraq. This is the same town where Jessica Lynch and her fellow soldiers were captured. Contrary to what Rubén Blades has asserted throughout the legal battle, I had no means to conduct any business from a combat zone. When asked in his deposition if he was aware that I was deployed to Iraq, he replied, "I don't care you were in Iraq, or you could have been at the end of the world. It's your name, it's your company."[2] So not having any means to conduct any business from a combat zone was no excuse, according to Rubén Blades. I was still responsible for the actions of the company, even though I had no control, access, or knowledge of what was going on.

One thing in particular that I find to be personally offensive is the fact that Rubén Blades and Ariel Rivas both stated many times in their testimonies and depositions that I had "disappeared," as if they had no knowledge that I was deployed to Iraq. Even though both Ariel Rivas and Arturo Martinez testified under oath that they had come to my house for a surprise farewell party my wife had for me prior to my deployment, and even though Rubén Blades knew since 2003 that I was, in fact, deployed, they still claim I disappeared. At the trial in 2013, more than ten years after I was deployed, Rubén Blades stated that I was "missing in action."[3]

What an offensive characterization, equating my being deployed to serve my country in a time of war as a reference to not being there for his damn *Siembra* concert. There are real soldiers that are and have been missing in action, who have paid the ultimate sacrifice while serving their country. He has no clue what that sacrifice means to the soldiers and their families. Yet he loosely references it to say that I was not available or somehow absent without his leave or approval. Sorry to disappoint, but my world does not now nor did it ever revolve around the whims and discretions of Rubén Blades. Looking back, I wonder if his seemingly callous response to my deployment could have been a reflection of his own experience with the US military presence in Panama during his youth.

While in Iraq, I served as the noncommissioned officer in charge (NCOIC) of the medical section for the 744th MP BN. My duties were to provide medical treatment to US forces, coalition forces, enemy prisoners of war, and displaced civilians caught up in the mess. I was responsible for a team of medics that carried out the same functions and duties.

We received and treated casualties of war every day. Sometimes they would come in by tens, twenties, or hundreds; some had minor wounds while others were in extremely serious conditions. Our supplies came up from Kuwait, but sometimes the main supply route would be compromised, and we would have to ration out our water and supplies. At one point in July of 2003, my commanding officer told me to pack up my gear and head south to Kuwait on the next convoy to try to get more medical supplies. While en route to Kuwait, I ran into a civilian contractor who had a satellite phone. This was the first time I was able to use a phone, but I had to pay for that privilege. It was not cheap, but when you're deployed out in the middle of the desert and it's your only opportunity for a call, money is not a concern. I was able to call my wife and see how she was doing. I also wanted to try to contact Arturo to see how he was doing. I just wanted to talk to someone back home. However, due to the time difference, it was very late back home. So I called someone I knew would be up at that hour—Tony Touch. He is a Latin hip-hop artist and producer, and he'd shared an office with us in New York

City. He picked up right away and during our conversation he told me that some shit had gone down with Arturo, but he didn't want to tell me what it was. I was very concerned, but he told me to contact Juan Toro. But that would have to wait until I had access to another phone.

Travel between my unit's location and Kuwait was often high risk, and convoys were delayed. I ended up staying in Kuwait for several weeks. The next opportunity I got, I found another satellite phone and contacted Juan Toro's office. Someone I knew very well answered the phone. She was also Arturo's friend. She realized it was me and began to laugh while telling me that Arturo had tried to kill himself and that my company was bankrupt. I can only assume by her smug attitude that she was relishing the moment. In this business, it is common to run into haters when you experience success, but I hadn't expected her to be one of those. I was upset. How could someone be so calloused as to laugh when saying that a mutual friend had tried to commit suicide?

I cut her off and asked to speak with Juan Toro, but he wasn't there. I can't remember if they patched me through to him or if I had to call again, but I was able to finally speak with him, and he told me what happened. He didn't get into any specific details. Instead, he told me to call Rubén. I tried several times to reach Rubén and even left a message at his house in Los Angeles. But it wasn't until sometime in September that I was able to reach him. When I spoke to him, he told me Arturo was in prison and monies were missing. I asked why Arturo was in prison, but Rubén told me to ask Juan Toro. I told him that I was still in Iraq, but that I would see if I could fix things when I returned. I gave him my lawyer's number in case he needed to contact me for anything, but he never did.

I didn't have all the details, but I knew there were big problems. My friend and business partner tried to kill himself and was in prison. My heart sank. There was nothing I could do—I was in Iraq and helpless to do anything back home.

Just writing these words today is hard for me to do: My friend had tried to commit suicide. Apparently, Arturo had kept everything inside for nearly three months, trying to manage a business that seemed to him to be plagued with debt and little resources, and hoping that something would happen to fix things. As he put it in his testimony at the default hearing, "I took an overdose of some pills, some sleeping pills. And I guess the pressure had gotten to me, and I wasn't strong enough to face the things, and you know, just wanted to sleep."[4] Arturo was hospitalized for ten days.

A few weeks later, Arturo met with Rubén Blades at Juan Toro's office to discuss the *Siembra* show. Desperate to come up with the money to pay Rubén Blades and Willie Colón, he decided to go to Panama and tried smuggling drugs into the United States. I want to emphasize here that Arturo is not a bad person. He had no previous experience dealing drugs. He had no criminal record. He was just someone caught up in a bad situation who made some wrong decisions. By August 22, 2003, Arturo was arrested and ultimately convicted of drug trafficking and sentenced to fifteen years in prison. I wish I could have been there for him. If I had not been deployed, he would never have gone to jail.

Once I was deployed, the affairs of the business rested squarely on the shoulders of Arturo Martinez. He was left to figure things out on his own with little preparation and practically no advance notice. This was without a doubt an enormous responsibility to thrust upon him. I knew it would be difficult for him, but I didn't think at the time that Arturo could not handle it. He was always a reassuring presence in the company. I could not have accomplished what I did without him. What I lacked in developing the business, he possessed. Together we made a great team that took our company from a start-up in 2000 to producing more than 60 percent of the Latin music concerts in New York City by the end of 2002. He was always there to count on. I was great at making the deals, and he was great at seeing them through.

But where I completely failed was in developing Arturo to replace me should anything happen to me. I seldom explained why I did things the way I did or what my strategy was or how I was accomplishing things. He knew the immediate plays but not the overall game plan. If there is one thing I learned from my deployment, it is the importance of building and training your team. In the army, leaders prepare those who are in the fight with them to take the lead and continue the mission should someone fall. Everyone knew the mission and the objectives. Everyone was trained and cross-trained. Everyone had the tools and equipment necessary to accomplish the mission, and most importantly, everyone was well aware and prepared for any possible challenges to come. Arturo was not given these valuable tools. He didn't have them because I failed to provide them.

At first it seems as though Arturo didn't miss a beat. He immediately started dealing on the *Siembra* show and apparently other planned events with Ariel Rivas. From the time the *Siembra* contracts were drafted until a few days before the *Siembra* concert, things were moving along as normal. Deposits were being made by the promoter, payments were being sent to Rubén Blades and Willie Colón, rehearsals were scheduled and conducted, flights were purchased, and hotel reservations were made. Every indication, at least on the surface, showed that things were all right. But they weren't.

The Early Years

Upper Left: On tour with Rubén Blades—backstage with Danny Glover and wife, Elaine Cavalleiro Glover, at the Crystal Ballroom; Portland, Ore., 1999.

Upper Right: With Cheech Marin—backstage at the James L. Knight Center; Miami, Fla., 1989.

Lower Left: With Bill Bellamy—backstage for the Russell Simmons Def Comedy Jam; UCF Arena, 1992.

Lower Right: On tour with Oscar D'León—Japan, 1994.

THE EARLY YEARS

Upper Left: With Victor Manuelle, Nelida Santa Rosa, Gilberto Santa Rosa, and Victor Colon—backstage at Madison Square Garden; New York, 1995*.

Upper Right: At my office with James Brown.

Middle Left: With (from left to right) Pupy Santiago, Wichy Camacho, Victor Manuelle, Giro, Juan Toro, Alex D'Castro, and David Maldonado—Salsa Mix Tour, 1995*.

Lower Left: On tour with Marc Anthony and fans—San Jose, Calif., 1994.

Lower Right: On stage with Victor Manuelle receiving first gold record—Madison Square Garden, New York, 1995*.

Photos By: Bernardo Tapia

THE APOLLO THEATER
(2002)

Upper Left: With Arturo Martinez

Upper Right: With Carlos Ponce

Lower Left: With Pablo Montero

Lower Right: With Chris Tucker

IRAQ & KUWAIT
(2003)

Upper Left: In Kuwait, June-July

Upper Right: Convoy mission near Baghdad, Iraq

Lower Left: Inside Saddam Hussein's Palace, Iraq

Lower Right: Heading out on a mission, Iraq

Iraq & Kuwait
(2003)

Upper Left: Breakfast in Bed, Iraq

Upper Right: In Kuwait, June-July

Lower Left: Saddam Hussein mural in Northern Iraq

Lower Right: Northern Iraq

16

COMING HOME

I WAS RELEASED FROM ACTIVE duty on July 3, 2004. It had been a year and a half since I was deployed. Nothing was the same as when I left, especially me. The business I built was gone. My friend was in prison. I had no money or ability to make any. But most significantly, I was broken inside. Nothing in the world could have prepared me for what I had experienced in Iraq. And nothing could have prepared me for my return. Getting deployed was actually easier than coming home. How do you come back from that? How do you just pick up the pieces as though nothing ever happened? How do you fit in with your own family, with your wife and kids? How do you reconcile with the things you had to do and had to witness? I didn't have the strength or the will to go back to the music business. Perhaps, this is what Rubén meant when he said I disappeared.

For the next eight months, I was a mess. I couldn't get it together. I kept thinking I was still in Iraq. I couldn't sleep. I kept thinking that if I fell asleep, someone was going to come and kill my family. No matter how hard I tried, I couldn't kick the fear. Every noise I heard was cause for panic. I checked the doors and windows constantly. I looked through the blinds. I guarded the house and my family as though I was still in that shithole. My mind was a constant battlefield. Two sides of me were fighting with each other: one side tried to reason that I was back home and everything was okay and we were safe, while the other side was convinced that as soon as I fell asleep, someone would break in and kill me and my family.

I isolated myself. I was distant with my family. I couldn't be in crowds. I couldn't stand loud noises. I was hypervigilant and distrustful. I experienced extreme rage, depression, and panic attacks. And when I did sleep, the nightmares were vivid and violent. I finally was able to suppress all of that. The best thing I could do was to keep myself as busy as possible so that I wouldn't dwell on the memories. I decided to get back into the army full time. I figured I could do that until I was ready to get back into the music business. It was always my intent to go back and pick up where I left off, but I needed time to integrate into my new reality.

I started working as an army recruiter in Pennsylvania in February 2005. I was on a three-year assignment, and my plan was to return to the music business after completing that tour. In 2006, I incorporated a new company called M&M Associates and Management Group with the expectation that when I left the army in 2008, I could start my business. However, that was not going to be possible. Sometime in May of 2007, I received a call from Luis Damon, the artist with whom I toured and made the cover of *Billboard* magazine. He told me he heard in the news that Willie Colón was suing Rubén Blades and that he thought it had something to do with the show Arturo was involved with in Puerto Rico. I could tell that he wanted to say more, but something was holding him back.

So when I hung up the phone, I did a Google search of *"Willie Colón demanda Rubén Blades."* To my surprise, several news articles popped up. The first one was from *People en Español (People Magazine)*. When I read the article, I was shocked to learn that Rubén Blades had accused me of stealing from him and Willie Colón. I kept reading everything that was out there, and all the articles said the same thing. It was carried on the newswires, Associated Press, and Internet sites all around the world. My name and reputation were tarnished. I knew that the statements made by Rubén Blades would keep me from ever getting back into the business.

I tried to contact Rubén in the hopes of clearing things up and letting him hear from me. I thought that if he said these things, it is probably because he was misinformed. He would not have made those statements if he did not believe them to be true, and he would not believe them to be true without a reason. I wanted to connect with him and present him with the full story. I didn't know where he was getting his information, but I knew I never took one cent from him.

My attempts at reaching him were unsuccessful. So I hired an attorney in Philadelphia. We sent him several letters via his office in the Department of Tourism for the Republic of Panama. Even those were unanswered. All we were asking for at that time was an audience with him to be able to talk about the matter and straighten things out. I was certain that if Rubén heard my side of things, he would realize that I had nothing to do with that event. But he never gave me that opportunity, the same opportunity he gave Arturo Martinez and Ariel Rivas. So, after ten months had passed without a response, I filed a lawsuit in New York for defamation against Rubén Blades.

My lawsuit against Rubén Blades was separate and apart from his lawsuit against Willie Colón. I had no cause to file anything against Willie Colón because he never accused me either publicly or in his lawsuit against Rubén Blades. My case against Rubén was being tried in New York, and Willie's case against Rubén was being tried in Puerto Rico. But that would all change.

17

DAVID AND GOLIATH

AS PART OF RUBÉN Blades' defense tactics with his case in Puerto Rico, he tried to get the case dismissed by claiming that Willie Colón failed to add indispensable parties. He claimed that Willie Colón should have included the company, Martinez, Morgalo & Associates, and me as defendants in the lawsuit against him, but because he didn't, the case should be dismissed. This tactic would have made the case go away if the court would have agreed with him and dismissed the case outright. Instead, the court ordered Willie Colón to amend his complaint and to add me and the company as defendants. Now I was brought into that lawsuit, even though Willie Colón had not accused me of anything. Willie has always maintained that he never dealt with me regarding the *Siembra* concert and that I was not a party to any of the negotiations or contracts for that event.

Now I was faced with a huge decision. I could not afford to fight two legal battles, one in New York and one in Puerto Rico. My choices were to either drop my defamation case and defend myself in the Puerto Rico case or move my defamation case to Puerto Rico and consolidate it with the Willie Colón case. I chose the latter, but it was not going to be easy. I could not afford an attorney—I was working full time and I was going to college full time. But I had no choice. I was not going to be branded a thief. I had to fight even if all the decks were stacked against me.

Rubén had a team of lawyers working for him, spearheaded by Pamela Gonzalez. She was an excellent attorney, very knowledgeable in the law, and extremely aggressive. She could hold her own against anyone. I was very impressed to the point that I told her that if my daughter became a lawyer, I would want them to meet.

I did not have a team of attorneys. In fact, once I moved my case to Puerto Rico, I had to resort to representing myself. This was a challenge to say the least. It was David and Goliath. I would get bombarded with motions, interrogatories, admissions, objections, and all sorts of legal papers—and all with specific deadlines for responses and rules of procedures that needed to be followed. I had no clue what to do or how to do it. If I was going to survive this, I would have to become a lawyer and fast. Google became my *consigliere*—my electronic advisor.

In 2008, the court in Puerto Rico gave permission for Rubén Blades and Willie Colón to depose Arturo Martinez in prison. This was the first time Arturo went on the record to discuss the case. When I saw his testimony, I couldn't believe what I was reading. I knew that he was either grossly misinformed or something was not right. I knew that what he was saying was not accurate. I couldn't explain it, but I had to find out. Something didn't add up.

It wasn't until two years later that I was able to subpoena his prison records. In those records I found some information that didn't sit well with me. Around the same time of his deposition, Juan Toro paid him a visit in prison. At that time, Juan Toro was Rubén Blades' agent. On the visitation form, Juan Toro is listed as Arturo's employer. Why would an agent of Rubén Blades go visit him around the same time as his deposition and be listed as the employer of the same person that supposedly stole money from Rubén Blades? Why was this not disclosed during his deposition? Why didn't anyone mention it at all until we brought it up at trial almost five years later? And why did Arturo Martinez walk out of prison and go straight to work for Juan Toro, Rubén Blades' agent?

I am not accusing anyone of anything. I have no knowledge of any quid pro quo or illicit motives. But as I said before, something just didn't feel right with me. Perception is everything, or so they say. You will see other instances in the chapters to come that will be just as difficult to comprehend as this. But that will have to wait for now.

18

WILLIE COLÓN'S DEPOSITION

IN APRIL OF **2009,** I had my first opportunity to confront Rubén Blades. There were depositions to be held in Puerto Rico with Willie Colón and Rubén Blades in connection with the claim Willie had filed against Rubén. The depositions were to take place over two days, back to back, with Willie Colón being deposed on the first day and Rubén Blades on the second. Although I was a party to the lawsuit because Rubén had brought me into it, I did not receive notification of the deposition from Rubén's attorney. It was Willie Colón's attorney, Juan Saavedra-Castro, who informed me. He felt it was only right that I would be given the opportunity to attend. I was very grateful that he did. If he hadn't informed me, I would never have known.

I gathered all of the evidence and documents I could find regarding the company, including every check ever written, every deposit received, every payment made, and every contract we'd ever engaged for our artists since the day we opened for business. I filled two huge suitcases with these items. I then flew to Puerto Rico and prepared for my first encounter with Willie and Rubén since my deployment in 2003.

It had been at least six years since I last saw them. To say I was nervous would be an understatement. Here I was at a deposition with two of the biggest names in Latin music and their respective attorneys, and I was there all alone. No law degree, no experience, and in way over my head. But I had to fight on. I didn't know how I was going to do this, but I knew I couldn't give up.

The first deposition was with Willie Colón. It was held in the offices of Rubén Blades' attorney. Rubén did not attend this deposition. I got there early and introduced myself to Pamela Gonzalez. She showed me to the conference room, and I brought in the two suitcases that had all the documents for the company. I sat there and waited until Willie Colón's attorney came in, and we introduced ourselves and shook hands. Then Willie came in. When he saw me he said, "Hello, Robert." He shook my hand and was very cordial. He made me feel at ease, and I realized that he had no problems with me. When the deposition started, I was sitting at the end of the table. Willie Colón and his attorney were to my left. To my right was Pamela Gonzalez. We were there all day and into the late afternoon. Ms. Gonzalez asked every question imaginable. I found Willie to be very credible in what he said. And I found it hard to believe that he would sue Rubén without cause. I believed that if he was suing Rubén, it was because he believed Rubén had promised to pay him.

There was evidence shown in that deposition that I had not seen before. One particular piece of evidence was a letter from Rubén Blades to Willie Colón, dated May 10, 2003 (see Appendix J). That letter was written shortly after the *Siembra* concert. In that letter, Rubén stated, "I told you I'd pay you because I feel morally obliged to do so. I'm not the agency, nor do I have the obligation legally to provide restitution to you. It's my choice because my integrity says it is the right thing to do." To me this was clear evidence that Willie Colón was saying the truth. That letter to me was a clear admission by Rubén Blades that he would pay Willie. I didn't understand the confusion. Maybe I was missing something. But from what I could see, that matter was indisputable. Why would Rubén say he had a moral obligation to pay if he did not agree to pay in the first place? And if he felt he had a moral obligation to pay Willie, why didn't he pay him?

Many times during the deposition, Rubén's attorney asked Willie about my involvement in the *Siembra* show. Willie responded every single time that I was never involved as seen in these excerpts from his deposition:[1]

> Ms. Gonzalez: Did he [Ariel Rivas] have an opportunity to tell you that he had negotiated the deal with Robert Morgalo?
>
> Willie Colón: No.
>
> Ms. Gonzalez: Did he tell you he negotiated....
>
> Willie Colón: As a matter of fact, to tell you the truth, I didn't even know that Morgalo was involved because I was only dealing with Martinez....
>
> Ms. Gonzalez: But, before you traveled to Puerto Rico, you knew that Robert Morgalo had disappeared to Iraq? Isn't that true?
>
> Willie Colón: I never even dealt with Robert Morgalo.

Willie Colón was getting irritated as Rubén's attorney continued to question him about my involvement, as seen in this exchange:

> Ms. Gonzalez: And what about Robert Morgalo?
>
> Willie Colón: I never even...he wasn't...to me, he was not part of this world here. He wasn't in this universe that I was in...you know...in this world of...his name was on some papers...you know...Martinez, Morgalo, but I never met with him, didn't speak with him.
>
> Ms. Gonzalez: But you knew he was a partner at this corporation?
>
> Willie Colón: Yeah, yeah, but he was not...apparently, he wasn't part of this deal.
>
> Ms. Gonzalez: Did Rubén Blades ask you not to press charges against Robert Morgalo?
>
> Willie Colón: No...when I learned that Arturo ran with the money, why am I going to press charges on Morgalo?

After Ms. Gonzalez finished her questioning, I had the opportunity to ask some questions of my own. I wanted to reaffirm what he had already stated to Ms. Gonzalez.

> Mr. Morgalo: And, the Engagement Contract, did Robert Morgalo have any dealings with you regarding this event?
>
> Willie Colón: None whatsoever....
>
> Mr. Morgalo: Okay, is Robert Morgalo's name anywhere present on that contract?
>
> Willie Colón: No, it is not....
>
> Mr. Morgalo: All right, in that verbal agreement that you and Blades made, was Robert Morgalo a party to that verbal agreement?
>
> Willie Colón: No.

I think that it is pretty clear from Willie Colón's testimony that I was not involved in the *Siembra* show—not in the negotiations and not in the contracts. So why was I being sued by Willie Colón? Because the judge ordered him to do that. And why did the judge so order? Because Rubén Blades had argued to the court that I should be included as a defendant. So I was being sued, not because Willie Colón believed I had done anything wrong, but because he had no choice. He'd been ordered to either include me or withdraw his lawsuit against Rubén Blades. I was brought into this case as a tactic by Rubén Blades, not because I was actually involved.

19

The Penny and the Truth

THE NEXT MORNING WAS the day for Rubén Blades' deposition. This was it—the day I would get to look him in the eye and let him know that I did not take anything from him and that I was not involved in the *Siembra* dealings. Today was the day that I would show him proof that I had been in Iraq and was unable to conduct any business from there. Once again, I was the first to arrive for the deposition. I did not want to be late and was anxious to get this started.

This time the deposition was held at the offices of Willie Colón's lawyer. Unlike the day before, both Willie Colón and Rubén Blades were present. Although I'd arrived early, I was not present when

Rubén and Willie arrived. I had stepped out for a moment. When I reentered the conference room, the lawyers were all there along with Willie and Rubén. I politely approached everyone, greeted them, and shook their hands. I thought it was the civil thing to do.

After shaking hands with Pamela Gonzalez, I extended my hand to Rubén Blades. His reaction was surprising and unbecoming a man of his stature. He immediately put both hands up in the air, backed up, and said, "No, no." I said, "No problem," and continued greeting the rest of the people in the room.

I couldn't believe that someone of Rubén Blades' intellect would act in such a childish and uncivil manner. This is the man who had run for the presidency of Panama, graduated from Harvard Law School, and garnered a reputation as an advocate for social justice. We were there in search of the truth in order to find a resolution. This was the first time we had seen each other since before I was deployed. It was an opportunity for him to ask me the same questions he had asked Arturo Martinez; the same questions he had asked Ariel Rivas. This was his time to confront me and hold me accountable. Yes, he was the one being deposed, not me. But I was there and willing to extend my hand to him even though he'd publicly accused me of stealing from him. I was available and willing to answer any of his questions. But he didn't even want to greet me, to extend a common courtesy or demonstrate civility. All of a sudden, I was the bigger man in the room. Not that I had elevated my own stature; rather, Rubén had lowered his.

Just as the day before, I was seated at the end of the table. The conference room was cramped and the table was overloaded with paperwork. Opposite me sat the reporter in charge of transcribing the deposition. To my right was Pamela Gonzalez, and on her right was Rubén Blades. To my left was Willie Colón, and on his left were his attorneys, Juan Saavedra-Castro and José A. Hernández-Mayoral.

The depositions had not even begun, and you could already feel the tension between Rubén's lawyer and Willie's lawyer. There seemed to be some underlying hostility masked within the context of their legal sparring. It was almost personal and, at some points, downright out of line.

It was all too surreal to me. I had waited for this moment since I'd first read Rubén's statements about me. I'd envisioned confronting him, showing him through my mere presence that I was not guilty of what he accused me of. I was not hiding from him; I was not ducking him. I was there because I wanted to be there. I was there because I wanted to look him in the eye so that he could see just who I am and what I am about.

My hands were sweaty, my legs were shaking, and my mind was racing. I had to calm down somehow. I put my hands in my pockets, and I felt a coin. I took it out, and it was a penny. I stared at that penny for a while. I tried to calm myself. I kept telling myself that everything would be okay. I told myself to focus on the truth, and if I got too overwhelmed, to focus on this penny. The penny was my reminder of the truth, and the truth was that I had never stolen a penny from them. No matter what happened, I could stand my ground as long as I stayed focused on that truth.

And so the deposition began.

> The Notary: Could you, please, raise your right hand and state your full name?
>
> The Deponent: Rubén Blades Vellido de Luna.

For the first part of the deposition, Willie Colón's attorney, Mr. Mayoral, deposed Rubén, although there were many interruptions and interactions between Juan Saavedra and Pamela Gonzalez that were almost comical at times. It ranged from the petty to the absurd to having to get the judge on the phone to resolve the squabbles that these two seasoned attorneys could not resolve for themselves. But this was all new to me. I had a front row seat, sitting at the adult table. However, I still felt like that kid from long ago—insecure, out of my league, and over my head. But fighting just the same. I was no attorney. I had no knowledge of the process or the law or the rules. The only training I had were shows like *Matlock, Perry Mason, A Few Good Men, Judge Judy,* and Google. But I had nothing left to lose.

Rubén was masterful in his responses. No one could take away from him his ability to capture a room. His answers were at once specific enough to be truthful yet vague enough to mean anything. One of his answers really surprised me. When asked when he met me, he said he thought it was either in the 1980s or 90s. He wasn't sure. How could he have worked with me for basically five years and not know when we met? Or what decade? Especially since he had enough years invested in this lawsuit to at least reflect on the chronology of the events leading up to the reasons why we were there in the first place.

In addition to his vagueness, he was careful with his answers, at times like a wordsmith parsing his words, while at other times somewhat careless and unguarded. It was in those careless and unguarded moments that I believe the real truth came out, not just some variation of the truth that was eloquently crafted in order to provide enough wiggle room to keep from being cornered.

Willie Colón's attorney questioned Rubén for several hours. Once he was finished, it was my turn to depose Rubén. I took my penny out of my pocket and placed it on the table in front of me. I was nervous but at the same time ready to do this. I asked for a few minutes to get my things in order. They asked me to switch places with Mr. Mayoral so that I could be in front of Rubén and next to the court reporter. I moved my paperwork and switched seats.

When we were getting ready to start I realized I'd left my penny on the table where I was sitting. I asked Mr. Mayoral to pass the penny over. He looked at me kind of dumbfounded, but he kindly obliged. It was one of those times where everyone looked around like "What the...?" It was an awkward, silent moment where I could tell that everybody wanted to know but no one dared to ask. I set the penny in front of me like a kid with his security blanket, took a deep breath, and began my questioning.

I had no idea that my first question to Rubén was going to be so contentious. Right away, Pamela Gonzalez objected. I insisted. The other attorneys tried to intervene. They almost called the judge. It was quite a spectacle, and it was just my first question. It was a simple yes or no question, but Rubén's attorney fought vigorously to keep him from answering it. The exchange went something like this:[1]

> Morgalo: Mr. Blades, do you believe that I stole money from you and [Willie] Colón?
>
> Gonzalez: Objection! That's not within the scope of the examination that counsel made.
>
> Morgalo: It is, because it pertains to everything that we're asking questions of here.
>
> Gonzalez: No. It pertains to your lawsuit against him for defamation.
>
> Morgalo: Which is consolidated.
>
> Gonzalez: But you need to depose him for that, because that's not the scope of this examination.
>
> Morgalo: Well, the objection is noted...Correct? [looking around for approval]
>
> Gonzalez: If you want to ask him questions about that, you need to schedule a deposition for the purposes of your lawsuit.

Morgalo: I asked him a question. The objection is noted. I just want to know if he can answer the question, if he believes that I stole money from him.

Gonzalez: Objection!

Saavedra-Castro [Willie Colón's attorney to Gonzalez]: Yes. But you are not going to instruct your client not to answer. I mean, because I'll call the judge.

Morgalo: The objection is noted?

Saavedra-Castro: Yes, the objection is noted.

Morgalo: The objection is noted.

Gonzalez: I don't believe you use this deposition to depose him on the substance of your claim against Mr. Blades.

Saavedra-Castro [to Gonzalez]: Counsel, your objection is noted.

Morgalo: It's noted.

Gonzalez: He does not need to answer that.

Saavedra-Castro: You want to call...?

Gonzalez: It's not relevant. It's not relevant to this.

Saavedra-Castro: Ok. The objection is noted.

Gonzalez: You can ask a question about the scope of his examination.

Hernández-Mayoral [Willie Colón's second attorney]: Quite Frankly, I don't know the answer to this, whether.... I mean to be honest, because he [Morgalo] is what? There is a cross-claim here?

Gonzalez: Correct.

Saavedra-Castro: Yes. And it's consolidated. It's all consolidated.

Gonzalez: It's a claim that he initiated in the Southern District of New York, it's a separate, different claim.

Hernández-Mayoral: Oh, it's a separate case.

Gonzalez: Yes, it is.

Morgalo: No. It's consolidated to this case!

Gonzalez: But it's a separate case. The cases are separate for the purposes of trial.

Saavedra-Castro: Pamela!

Gonzalez: Counsel, let me finish!

Saavedra-Castro: Oh. I thought you had finished.

Gonzalez: Your case against my client is a separate and distinct matter that is not going to be tried together with this case.

Morgalo: Well, just so you understand, the numbers and the figures that Rubén Blades is addressing here...are the same numbers and figures, and he said, in this particular case, in this statement...he said that we stole from him.

Blades: Yes.

Gonzalez: No he did not.

Morgalo: He said it in this.... Hold a second [looking around and fumbling through the evidence]. He said it in this particular deposition.

Gonzalez: No he did not.

Morgalo: Yes he did. And we can go back to the record.

Gonzalez: Not in this deposition.

Morgalo: In this deposition, he said it several times.

Gonzalez: Secondly, it's immaterial....

Morgalo: It's in the record [still looking through the evidence].

Gonzalez: Excuse me! What he believes about what you did, or what your partner did, or the corporation did is immaterial to this case.

Morgalo: But in all the...exhibits that are presented here as evidence... all right? It states on...

Saavedra-Castro: Let's call the Judge,

Gonzalez: What he believes is immaterial.

Saavedra-Castro:	*Sí, pero es que me molesta el abuso.* [Yes, but it's just that the abuse bothers me.]
Morgalo [to Saavedra-Castro]:	I appreciate that. [Then to all]: Look, exhibit 13, which is part of the record here, of this deposition, it says: "I also want Arturo to clarify the extent of Robert Morgalo's involvement in this situation, and because so far, Arturo is the one we all have focused on, but it seems to me, it's obvious, Morgalo had a hand as well in the embezzlement, and it's in Arturo's personal interest to explain what role the latter played in this." This was not just entered into evidence, but it was stated verbally.
Gonzalez:	That's fine. You may ask a question about that exhibit.

Finally! All this back and forth to get my first question answered by Rubén Blades. It seemed pretty straightforward. Did he believe that I stole money from him and Willie Colón or not? I couldn't understand the hesitation or deliberate resistance to answering such a simple question.

What were they afraid of? He had no problem writing a letter to Willie Colón stating that I had stolen money from him when I was not around to defend myself. Now, when confronted with the question by me, we had to jump through all these hoops just to get him to answer the question. Imagine that. Rubén had a team of highly paid attorneys, and all I had was Google and *Matlock*, and I was able to overcome all the objections and legal posturing just so Rubén could say yes.

It later became apparent to me why Ms. Gonzales did not want Rubén to answer that question: It put him in a position where he would be held accountable for those same words. Those exact words came back to haunt him at the defamation trial. His main defense was that he never accused me personally, and that at all times, he was just referring to the company. But it was clear here that he was talking about me.

I went on to ask him many questions during this deposition with somewhat similar exchanges and outcomes—far too many to include in this book. But one thing that I think must be shared can be seen in this exchange:[2]

> Morgalo: Do you believe that if it is proven that Robert Morgalo stole money, and embezzled money from both you and Colón, that Robert Morgalo should be held accountable for it?
>
> Blades: I think Morgalo and Martinez should be held accountable for it....
>
> Morgalo: Okay. I am asking specifically about Robert Morgalo.
>
> Blades: I am answering you the office.... To me, Robert Morgalo is one of the two people that were involved in this issue. We're talking about the office of Martinez and Morgalo. I'm not making this personal.
>
> Morgalo: Okay.
>
> Blades: As a member of that office, you are either solidary, or you have a responsibility in what happened. That's my position.
>
> Morgalo: Okay. In the same token, if it is proven that Robert Morgalo had no embezzlement, and Robert Morgalo did not steal money, should Robert Morgalo, in the same token...be held responsible.... Can Robert Morgalo be exonerated?
>
> Gonzalez: Objection! That is a legal question.
>
> Blades: I have no idea. Because that would be up to a judge...not me.

There are several issues that I would like to point out in this last exchange. First, if Rubén felt that both Arturo and I should be held accountable, then why did he only sue me and prosecute his case against only me and the company? Not only did Rubén not sue Arturo, but when I tried to add Arturo into the case, Rubén filed motions defending him and keeping him from being added to the case, as you will see later on.

Second, why is it *not* a legal question when it comes to finding me accountable if it is proven that I stole money, but it *is* a legal question if it is proven that I did not steal any money? Rubén's testimony here is just hypocritical, and it's a double standard. But most importantly, it reflects on how the process of litigation can make even the most reasonable and intellectual of men apprehensive to commit to what would seem the correct and appropriate response.

20

Lift, Shift, and Adjust

AFTER WE FINISHED THE deposition, I got the impression that Rubén was beginning to see that the information he had come to believe was somehow not adding up. He was still unwilling to acknowledge it, but he did inform me afterward that he would look into these things and hopefully we could resolve it and he would be willing to shake my hand. I told him I didn't need him to shake my hand; I needed him to believe I never stole anything from him. I left that deposition feeling good. I felt good that I was able to show him things he hadn't known. I thought that this might be a turning point. Most importantly, I was hopeful for the first time that Rubén would realize the truth. But those expectations would be short lived.

Rubén's attorney kept bombarding me with legal papers and deadlines. She asked me to sign a waiver for the company. I didn't know why because the company had been closed for more than five years by then. But I did. It turned out to be a waiver of service, so that they could sue the company. I didn't care; the business was closed. But that decision turned out to be leverage for Rubén Blades. They filed for a default judgment on the company. Since there was no one representing the company, they won their claim by default. Not on merits, but by default. It's like playing a soccer match and the other team doesn't show up. There was no defense for the company because it had been closed for more than five years. Yet they took that waiver and had a hearing before the Honorable Justo Arenas.

It would be another year before that hearing would take place—another year of legal wrangling, motions, affirmative responses, rules, procedures, and deadlines. I could not go another year representing myself. I had to do something. I needed to hire an attorney, and I needed to raise some funds. But how? I was working full time with the army, going to college full time, and dealing with all of these court proceedings.

Then one day my father called to tell me that there was someone trying to get hold of me to put together a tour. It was a representative for a group from Cuba that had defected to the United States in 2008. They wanted to know if I could put together a tour for their group, similar to what I had done for Luis Damon. I was not willing to do it because I had my hands full. So I told them that I would need to be paid for my services up front. I gave them a price of $20,000, thinking they wouldn't accept it. However, they agreed; and with that I was able to raise the funds to retain an attorney. But now

I had to put together a tour. I had not done that in years, and with everything that was going on in my life at the time, I was unsure if I could get it done. It took every moment I could spare to put that tour together. It turned out to be a six-week tour across the country. The tour had its share of problems, mostly with logistics, the types of venues booked, and the expectations of the group. But I did my part. I booked the dates, the group toured, and I had the money to retain an attorney.

To be honest, I can't remember how I came to find my attorneys. I had tried so many attorneys in Puerto Rico, and each referred me to someone else. I went through a few rounds of that before I was finally referred to Juan Frontera-Suau and Israel Alicea. It turns out they had a clear understanding of my case and the relevant case law, and they were always straight with me as to what my chances were and the difficulties we would face.

They agreed to take the case, and I finally had some peace of mind, knowing I had experienced lawyers on my side. They went to work immediately on my behalf. The first order of business was to prepare for the default hearing against the company. They were not representing the company, just me in my personal capacity and my best interest at that hearing. Their focus there was to defend me against the cross claims filed against me by Rubén Blades and to advance and prosecute my defamation claim against him.

And then, prior to the default hearing—on March 31, 2010, to be exact—I faced a huge legal setback. Judge Justo Arenas dismissed my defamation claim against Rubén Blades. I had been aware that Rubén Blades' attorney had filed a motion to dismiss, but I was completely shocked by the decision. To give you a better understanding of how the court made its decision, let me explain the order of events that led to Pamela Gonzalez filing the motion to dismiss and ultimately the court's decision to dismiss my case.

Remember that during the depositions of both Willie Colón and Rubén Blades in the early part of 2009, I had brought two suitcases with me, filled with company documents. At both depositions, the lawyers were on record acknowledging that I had brought those documents and that they were going to review them and make copies as necessary.[1,2] So in good faith and having nothing to hide, I left all of those original documents with Willie Colón's attorney. Then in September 2009, my newly hired attorneys, along with the attorneys for the other parties met with Judge Arenas to go over the proceedings, discovery rules, and trial calendar. It was agreed at that meeting that we would be able to depose all of the parties specifically for the defamation case and that we would continue in the discovery process.

The parties agreed that the dates for the depositions would be in February 2010. Rubén's attorney had requested that I produce the documents that I turned over at the depositions earlier that year. I had no possession of them. I asked that they be turned over to her, but the attorneys for Willie Colón had misplaced them and could not find them. I even flew down to Puerto Rico to try to locate them but was unsuccessful. I was served a second set of interrogatories on January 22, 2010. I had until February 22, 2010, to answer those interrogatories. (Interrogatories are a set of questions that one party presents to the other. Parties are required to provide answers to the interrogatories.)

During this process, Rubén Blades' attorney threatened to not have Rubén attend his scheduled deposition in February because I had "refused" to turn over the documents that had been lost or misplaced by Willie Colón's attorneys, and because I had not yet answered the second set of interrogatories.

We complied; however, my attorneys filed the material three days past the deadline. On the same day, Rubén's attorney filed the motion to dismiss, and eight days later the judge granted them their dismissal. To add insult to injury, I was fined $1,000 by the court for failing to produce the box of documents that Willie Colón's attorneys had misplaced. Rubén's attorney also filed a motion to preclude me from using any of those documents as evidence in my defamation case. I paid that $1,000 fine immediately, and then the judge granted their request to not allow me to use any of those documents as evidence. Think about that. We were supposed to search for and find the truth, but Rubén's attorney didn't want those documents to be admitted in court.

Shortly after my case was dismissed, Willie's attorneys found the boxes with the missing documents. I do believe that it was an honest mistake and not done intentionally. They had moved some offices, and the boxes were lost in the mix. Willie's lawyer filed an informative motion with the court, explaining what happened and taking responsibility for the misplaced documents. We then filed a motion to reconsider, but the judge was not moved. I still had to pay the fine and was prohibited from using any of those documents in my case. Where was the justice?

21

ON THE RECORD

To have my defamation case against Rubén Blades dismissed was beyond comprehension. My attorneys were just as surprised. We had answered the second set of interrogatories, and we had complied with the production of all evidence within our control. I had handed all the original documents to seasoned attorneys in good faith and with nothing to hide, and I had no control over them. Yet the court determined me to be noncompliant, fined me $1,000, and now my defamation claim was dismissed and I was not allowed to use any of those documents. This was just more ammunition for Rubén to use in the media, but more importantly, it was a huge emotional setback for me.

I was drained, depressed, angry, and I felt almost hopeless. I was fighting as hard as I could, but it seemed like everything was against me, like it was rigged. Not only was I fighting the legal battle in the courts, I was also fighting my own battles at home. My family and close friends too often would say, "Just let it go." "It doesn't matter." "Who cares what people think."

I know that they were trying to help, trying to comfort me and make me feel better. But I felt they didn't understand. What would you do if everybody thought you'd stolen money from someone, and you knew you hadn't?

I filed an appeal. Our claim on the appeal was that the judge had abused his discretion, which is something very hard to prove. It is my belief that this judge was biased, based on my observations and how he spoke and interacted with Rubén Blades. He seemed to me to be easily moved by Rubén's motions but kept denying mine. Still, I had not expected anything like this. The appeal would take another two years to resolve. Meanwhile, we still had the default hearing to contend with and Rubén's cross claim against me.

Because I was not a party to the default hearing against the company, I was not allowed to cross-examine any of Rubén Blades' witnesses. I was not allowed to confront them or dispute their testimony. It was a one-sided argument. When I arrived at the courtroom with my attorneys, I found Ariel Rivas, Rubén Blades, and Arturo Martinez there, all sitting together. The media was there as well. I entered and sat at the back of the courtroom. I informed my lawyers that Arturo was there. I hadn't known he was out of prison or that he would be there as a witness for Rubén Blades. My attorneys jumped into action immediately.

Israel Alicea left the courtroom to file a summons on a third-party complaint against both Arturo Martinez and Ariel Rivas. Basically, this would be the paperwork needed to include them as defendants in the lawsuit. By the time they left the courtroom for the lunch recess, both Ariel Rivas and Arturo Martinez had been served with their summons.

Meanwhile in the courtroom, Juan Frontera stayed to look after my interest in the case. The atmosphere in the courtroom was like a scene at a backstage party. The court reporter, bailiff, and other people in the room were taking pictures with Rubén, laughing and asking for autographs.

Although I was called to testify, my answers were extremely limited. I was unable to deviate from the leading questions presented to me.

Rubén Blades, Arturo Martinez, and Ariel Rivas all testified, but none of them were cross-examined. They were unchallenged in their testimonies. They had no opposition, because the company being sued was closed. There was no defense, and since I was just a witness and not a party, I could not challenge them. The only witness who was cross-examined and reexamined was me.

While I was testifying, Rubén's attorney tried many times to connect me to the *Siembra* concert dealings.[1] She kept asking leading questions that implied that I had agreed to or negotiated the *Siembra* contract, or that I had agreed to apply the $62,500 from the 2002 Rubén Blades contract to the 2003 *Siembra* contract. And every time, I answered with the same response: a resounding no. I realize now that the reason she grilled me so much on this point is because she had absolutely no proof.

What we did have was testimony by Rubén Blades that he had never authorized such a transfer. In his testimony at the default hearing against the company of Martinez, Morgalo & Associates, Rubén Blades was asked, "Did you authorize or consent to the application of $62,500 as deposit for a *Siembra* concert from another show of yours?" Rubén replied, "Never!"[2]

So if he didn't authorize it, and I didn't authorize it, then where did he come up with his assertion that those funds were to be applied from one show to the other? The answer can be found in the transcripts of his deposition, the one where I was deposing him and had to fight tooth and nail just to get some answers. I had asked Rubén, "What gives you the impression that those $62,500 were to be applied toward the *Siembra* show?" Rubén's response to me was, "I get it from the promoter."[3] In this case, the promoter was Ariel Rivas of Dissar Productions.

So it was clear to me that Rubén's entire understanding and characterization of these events were formulated by the information that was given to him initially by Ariel Rivas and subsequently by Arturo Martinez. This perspective was not determined by facts or subject to any opposing information or adequate scrutiny of the information being presented. I was not there to counter those claims at the time that Rubén was receiving them. What else could Rubén have done at the time, except to believe what he was being told?

None of the parties involved—not Rubén, not Arturo, and definitely not me—had authorized such a transfer for the reallocation of the Rubén Blades' concert funds to the *Siembra* show as testified by all three parties.[4,5,6] The only person making the claim that I had authorized the $62,500 to be applied toward the *Siembra* contract was Ariel Rivas—who, incidentally, was the only person who would benefit from such a transfer.[7] The contract that was entered into evidence was clear: "Any cancellation by the promoter would result in a forfeit of deposit" (see Appendix A). Additionally, there was nothing submitted into evidence showing that I had authorized the reallocation of those funds to the *Siembra* show.

When the hearing was over, the media swarmed outside the federal courthouse, waiting for Rubén Blades. Rubén was all too available to speak with them. None of them approached me with a single question. The next day the newspapers, radio stations, and Internet sites were full of Rubén Blades' comments and his version of what had transpired. He used Arturo Martinez' testimony as the smoking gun to further advance his claims. Arturo Martinez had admitted on the witness stand to mismanaging the funds,[8] and Rubén was milking it for all it was worth. Yet no one could cross-examine him. Arturo's testimony was unchallenged, as was the testimony of Ariel Rivas.

It was evident to me at this point that Rubén had a huge advantage when it came to public perception. He was a celebrity with access to the press and an uncanny ability to frame the dialog to his advantage. He was, after all, Rubén Blades. I had no such voice. I didn't have the ability to reach millions of people around the world in just one interview. If I wanted to be heard, I would have to score a victory.

The good thing about the hearing is that I was finally able to go on the record. I was able to present the fact that I was deployed when the dispute occurred, that I was not a party to the contracts, and that I did not authorize the transfer of those funds. I had also served Arturo Martinez and Ariel Rivas each with a third-party summons and complaint, requesting to add them as defendants to the lawsuit.[9,10]

Interestingly, Rubén Blades, through his attorney, Pamela Gonzalez, opposed us and filed a motion to keep them from being sued. Imagine that. Arturo Martinez admitted in court to mismanaging the funds, yet Rubén Blades was actively defending him from being sued. Why? He'd had no problem adding me to the lawsuit. And it isn't just that he didn't file a lawsuit himself against Arturo Martinez or Ariel Rivas; it's that he actually went into action and had his attorney file motions to defend them.[11]

Once again, Judge Justo Arenas' partiality was displayed. He granted Rubén's motion to keep Arturo Martinez and Ariel Rivas from being sued. I could not understand it. Rubén asked the court to add me as a defendant to the case, and the judge granted it. I asked the court to add Arturo and Ariel as defendants, and the court denied it, even after hearing Arturo himself on the witness stand, saying that he'd mismanaged the money.

22

STOP THE PRESSES

THAT DEFAULT HEARING WAS in April 2010. Although there was not a whole lot of court action after that, there were plenty of fireworks in the court of public opinion. In the beginning of May, Willie Colón announced that he had dismissed his lawsuit because there was a settlement. The media assumed that he had resolved the matter with Rubén, and that Rubén had paid him off.

This made Rubén upset, and he put out press releases and made public announcements stating that the deal reached was between Willie Colón and me. He further stated that reaching an out-of-court settlement proved I was involved. Once again, the media was all over it, and I was helpless to do or say anything about it. His statements were carried around the globe, but no one contacted my attorneys or me for a rebuttal. Whatever Rubén Blades said, they published and left it at that.

The fact is that I never paid off anyone. I received an e-mail from my lawyers on May 4, 2010. The subject of the e-mail caught me completely by surprise, and at first I was furious. It was a settlement offer from Willie Colón. The offer was for me to pay Willie a sum of money on behalf of the company, but only if Rubén Blades agreed to dismiss all claims with prejudice against me in my personal capacity.

I called my lawyer and he got an earful from me. I was livid. Why would I pay anyone for something I hadn't done or had anything to do with? After I hung up and had time to calm down, I started reflecting on this offer—not as an ultimatum or an insult, but rather as an opportunity.

I wasn't suing Rubén for the money. I was suing for my reputation. If I could find a middle ground where I could get my reputation back and help them recover their money, then I would be able to get back to doing what I loved. But I was not going to pay anyone out of my pocket. So I called my attorney and presented a counter offer of my own.

I proposed that the amount of money Willie Colón was willing to accept as a settlement was too little for what he'd actually lost. I offered that he should get double that amount and that Rubén Blades should get the same amount. But my conditions were that the money did not come from my pocket, because I didn't owe anyone anything.

What I proposed was that both Willie and Rubén allow me to book some of their dates and that the commission for the work I performed would be split in half—one half for them and one half for me. This way it would not be coming out of my pocket. They would get their money, we could resolve the claims, and I would be established back into the music business. But both Willie Colón and Rubén Blades had to agree to those terms.

So, I presented this offer, and the next thing I heard was the press already reporting that Willie and Rubén had reached an agreement. However, Rubén adamantly denied it. In fact, he did not accept the deal I'd proposed at all. Nonetheless, Willie Colón voluntarily dismissed all his claims against Rubén Blades and me, with prejudice. The only claims remaining were Rubén's cross claim against me in my personal capacity and my claim against him for defamation, which was being appealed. This was in May 2010.

The trial for Rubén's cross claim against me was scheduled to begin in June at the Federal Court of Puerto Rico, before the Honorable Justo Arenas. I flew down with my wife, even though I was still recovering from the second of three reconstructive surgeries on my right ankle due to injuries from my deployment. I was moving about on a knee walker; a little scooter you push yourself around on instead of using crutches. My close friend, Agustine "Tony" Carreras, was also there for support. This was the day that Rubén Blades would proceed with his claims against me; the day he could present all of his evidence supporting his assertions that I had done something wrong.

Keep in mind, Willie Colón's case was already dismissed. This was my opportunity to challenge Rubén Blades' claims and accusations against me. This was his time to put up or shut up. They could present any evidence against me and call up their witnesses; only this time, they would be cross-examined and their evidence put to scrutiny. And then, at the opening of the trial, Rubén's attorney requested that she be allowed to use the documents that she had fought so hard to keep me from using in my defense in order to prove their case.

Apparently, they didn't have any evidence. If they had, they would have proceeded with the trial. Rubén didn't want the judge to allow me to enter those documents as evidence in my defense, but he had no problem asking the judge to allow him to use them. And once again, the judge granted Rubén's request. As a result, my trip to Puerto Rico just a few weeks after my surgery was all for nothing. The trial was postponed, because Rubén needed more time to prove his case.

Over the next few months, there were more legal maneuvers between Rubén's attorney and my attorneys. We were able to start our discovery as to Rubén Blades' claims against me. We deposed Arturo Martinez on May 18 and Rubén Blades on May 19, 2010. I was deposed on May 20. Ariel Rivas had already been deposed earlier in February as scheduled. So now we had the testimonies of all involved, and we were able to move forward. On top of that, we were now able to use the documents I had brought down with me in those two suitcases back in 2009.

Two pivotal things happened during this time. First, we were able to establish that Rubén Blades did not have standing to sue me. When a case comes before a court, the person or party making the claim must have a real, legal standing to bring the claim. If that party does not have standing, then the court does not have jurisdiction or authority to hear the case or make any ruling on the subject matter. This is a constitutional issue and one that is quite clear with plenty of legal precedent. Second, I finally had a victory—albeit a small one—to release to the press.

Using the documents the judge had previously precluded, I was able to show that all monies pertaining to every event, concert, and dealings with Rubén Blades had gone to his company, Rubén Blades Productions, and not to Rubén Blades himself. We further proved that all of the monies received for any of Rubén's shows or dealings had gone to the company Martinez, Morgalo & Associates, and never to me individually. We were also able to prove that all monies transferred from the company Martinez, Morgalo & Associates had gone to Rubén Blades Productions, and not Rubén Blades personally. Finally, with Arturo's testimony at the default hearing, we were able to establish that I had had no access to any of the money once I was deployed.[1] So as a matter of law, Rubén Blades had no standing in this case. The court determined that Rubén Blades did not possess a legal right to bring a claim against me.

Yet, instead of dismissing the case altogether, as should be done when a court lacks jurisdiction, the Honorable Justo Arenas simply ordered the wording changed: "Rubén Blades"—the person—was to be substituted by "Rubén Blades Productions." Basically, even though Rubén Blades had no standing and the court had no jurisdiction or authority to hear the case or rule on its merits, the judge once again displayed favoritism. He could and should have dismissed the claim altogether, but he didn't.

Even so, we had turned a corner. This was my first victory. I had something to say, and I said it. I hired a publicist and published my first press release. The headlines were very positive, and for the first time I was able to present the other side of this dispute. When the media started covering my side of the case, Pamela Gonzalez e-mailed my attorneys to find out why I was making statements to the press. Imagine that. For the past three to four years, Rubén Blades had made countless statements to the press. I maintained silence through all of them. But when I finally had something to say in my defense in the court of public opinion, Pamela Gonzalez wrote to my lawyer: "Juan, Are you still representing Mr. Morgalo in this litigation? Why is he making statements to the press and did you authorize them?"[2] It seems as though I struck a nerve. I was not just a punching bag any more. I was hitting back, and they didn't like it.

23

A SHIFT IN THE CURRENT

I HAD SCORED A SMALL victory; the playing field in the media, although still not level, was now at least somewhat accessible. The court's decision that Rubén Blades had no standing to sue me was issued on September 2, 2010.[1] This decision was not well received by Rubén. His attorney filed a motion for reconsideration and amended the complaint. However, they did not follow the judge's order. Instead of substituting "Rubén Blades" with "Rubén Blades Productions," they amended their complaint by simply adding Rubén Blades Productions as a co-plaintiff and leaving Rubén Blades' name in the claim.

It seemed that Rubén did not want to be forced out of the lawsuit. He just didn't get it. He had no standing to sue me. I am not a lawyer, but I understood this simple premise. If you have no standing, you cannot sue. The motion they filed for the judge to reconsider his decision and to allow Rubén Blades to stay on as a plaintiff was emphatically denied.[2]

I was now accumulating some victories; however, none that I could take to the media. These small legal victories had no substantial impact for the press to report. But they were impacting the direction of the case. Rubén was no longer getting his way with the rulings. There was a definite shift in the current, and it seemed like these little setbacks for Rubén were coming more frequently.

In an interview with the news agency *Primera Hora*, under the title *"Rubén Blades Se Desahoga"* or "Rubén Blades Vents," it was obvious by his demeanor that we were getting under his skin.[3] This interview was posted December 15, 2010, shortly after the judge's order that Rubén had no standing. Even in this interview, Rubén was reluctant to accept the fact that he had no standing. He went even further in his accusations by stating it was ridiculous that I had sued him for defamation but I hadn't sued my partner. "Why didn't he sue his partner?" he asked. "I'll tell you why he didn't sue him. Because everything would be known." How could he state publicly that I hadn't tried to sue my partner, when I did in fact attempt to sue Arturo Martinez, but Rubén himself had filed a motion to keep me from doing so?[4,5] Once again, Rubén had the advantage of being a celebrity—every word he said could be published without anyone verifying the information.

After the court ruled that Rubén Blades had no standing to sue me, I was feeling pretty generous. I realized that this would be a good opportunity to put all this legal mess behind us. So I told my attorneys to present Rubén with an offer: I proposed that we mutually drop all of the pending cases and just walk away. I was willing to let it go if he was. But the response from Rubén's attorney reflected the pride and stubbornness that drove his decisions.

Pamela Gonzalez' response was short and to the point: "My clients are not interested in agreeing to terms that afford them no measure of justice. Therefore, they decline your settlement offer." Notice how she used the plural when referring to her "clients."[6] The court had already ruled that Rubén Blades had no standing. My offer was with respect to Rubén Blades Productions, and I was willing to withdraw my defamation case against Rubén. But they were bent on making me personally responsible.

Then, on December 28, 2010, just eighteen days after turning down my offer, there was a significant setback for Rubén Blades. This time it was substantial enough to grab the media's attention. Back on July 13, 2010, Rubén's lawyer had filed a cross-motion for summary judgment.[7] This is a motion telling the court that they had proven their case based on the evidence of discovery. It took almost six months for the court to make its decision on this motion, and it was not favorable at all for Rubén Blades. They tried to use the fact that the court had granted them a judgment against the company as a basis for their request for summary judgment against me. The court not only denied Rubén's motion, it clearly spelled out the reasons and completely rebuked the claims that Rubén Blades had made against me all this time. The court concluded that, "There is no evidence that Morgalo committed fraud" and "Cross-plaintiff (Rubén Blades) submits no proof of fraud before this Court" and yet again, "Cross-Plaintiff fails to point this Court to anywhere in the record with evidence that MM&A (Martinez, Morgalo & Associates) or Morgalo committed fraud."[8] This last remark was particularly favorable to me, because it not only showed that I had not committed the fraud that Rubén was accusing me off, it also made it clear that the company had not committed fraud as well. Remember, Rubén Blades won a default judgment against the company in May 2010 because there was no challenge to his case since the company was closed. Rubén had continuously referenced that judgment in the press, claiming that the judge had awarded him $133,000 in damages. Now that there was a challenge from me, the court was able to see that not even the company had done anything wrong.

This was huge. It was a great belated Christmas gift. I was ecstatic. I contacted my publicist and started working on a press release shortly after the New Year. It was now 2011, and the year was beginning to look great. The original judge in the case was retiring, and we were getting a new one. My appeal was already with the First Circuit Court of Appeals in Boston waiting on a decision, and I had a press release ready to go out. Things were not as one-sided as they once were. I couldn't help but think just how shortsighted and stubborn Rubén was. He could have accepted my offer a couple of weeks earlier, and he would have saved himself this embarrassment. Imagine, all this time he had been accusing me publicly, and now the court had ruled that he had no proof of what he was claiming against me.

The new judge was the Honorable Bruce J. McGiverin. I traveled to Puerto Rico to meet with my attorneys and had a chance to see this judge in court on other federal cases. I was impressed with his fairness, his treatment of the defendants, his explanations of the law, his judgment, and his overall presence. I knew then that whatever he decided on my case, it would be fair.

24

Rubén Loses the Case

ALTHOUGH **2011** STARTED OUT looking bright, it was mostly uneventful—just more waiting on the appeal and other legal procedures, and not much in the way of progress with the case. The press had covered the setbacks suffered by Rubén Blades in the earlier part of the year, but the rest of the year just seemed to drag on. I was anxious and constantly bothering my lawyers. I knew I was annoying, but I just couldn't help it. I e-mailed and called, and most of the time didn't get a response. Not because they were being rude or anything, but because I had become "that guy." The one who calls for any little thing that pops into his mind.

To say that this case consumed me is an understatement. I was glued to the computer, researching other court cases and decisions similar to mine. Constantly checking to see if there was any change in the status of my appeal. This period of time was one of the hardest for me. I wanted resolution of this matter, and I am not a patient person by nature. I am not the type to wait for something to happen—I'm usually the one who makes things happen.

As the end of the year drew closer, I began to experience deep depression and anxiety. I began to lose hope of ever getting my reputation back and being able to get back into the music business. The effects of being ostracized from those I knew in the industry, the shame I felt from the accusations and attacks on my character, and the fatigue of fighting this battle for so long were taking their toll.

Then, on December 27, 2011, I had a resounding victory. There were three motions, among others, that were filed in 2011. One of them was another motion filed by Rubén Blades for summary judgment against me. The other two were motions from me—a motion to dismiss for lack of subject matter jurisdiction, and a motion for summary judgment against Rubén Blades Productions.

The judge ruled that Rubén Blades' motion for summary judgment was denied and that my motion to dismiss for lack of subject matter jurisdiction was also denied. However, my motion for summary judgment against Rubén Blades was granted. I was beside myself with shock when I read the decision. I couldn't believe what I was reading. Was I reading it right? Was I missing something? This time it was a fatal blow to Rubén Blades' case against me. This time it was final. I won!

Not only was the court's language in the decision very favorable to me and my reputation, but it was particularly stinging for Rubén Blades. The court stated, "RBPI's [Rubén Blades Production, Inc.'s] pleadings and motions are not a model of clarity, and it takes some effort to discern what its theories of recovery are." However, the court determined that, "Read generously, RBPI moves for summary judgment on four grounds: (1) that Morgalo is liable for breach of contract; (2) that Morgalo is liable for breach of fiduciary duty as an agent; (3) that Morgalo breached a duty as an MM&A officer; and (4) that Morgalo should be held personally responsible for MM&As judgment by piercing the corporate veil."[1]

As for the breach of contract claim (1), the judge stated, "As Morgalo points out, RBPI offers no evidence showing that Morgalo was a party to the contracts for either the *Siembra* concert or the Cheo concert" (the December 2002 concert). Further, "RBPI has offered no evidence of this and is therefore not entitled to judgment on this theory."[2]

As for the breach of duty as Rubén Blades' agent (2), the judge ruled as follows, "RBPI argues in its motion for summary judgment that Morgalo breached a duty he owed as Blades' agent. As Morgalo persuasively points out, however, RBPI has not brought forth any evidence that Morgalo personally acted as an agent for either Blades or RBPI. Specifically, RBPI offers no evidence showing that Morgalo accepted a role as Blades' agent in his personal capacity…. Because RBPI has not presented evidence of any agency relationship between Morgalo and Blades or RBPI, it is not entitled to summary judgment on this theory."[3]

As to the breach of duty as an officer of MM&A (3), this is somewhat of a more nuanced legal issue. The judge concluded: "Applying Puerto Rico law, I find that RBPI has not shown Morgalo, as opposed to MM&A, to be subject to preexisting obligation, and therefore the cause of action arises under Article 1802." He closed out this section with, "Because the *Siembra* deal took place in 2003… and RBPI has proffered no evidence to meet its burden, RBPI is not entitled to summary judgment on this claim."[4]

Finally, as to holding Morgalo personally liable and piercing the corporate veil (4), this is what the judge had to say: "RBPI is not entitled to judgment because Morgalo has proffered evidence creating a genuine dispute as to whether MM&A was adequately separate from himself." Therefore, "RBPI is not entitled to summary judgment."[5]

Although the judge denied Rubén's summary judgment, he granted mine on the same basis. He ruled that, "For the reasons discussed above, Morgalo has established that he cannot be held directly liable for the Cheo or *Siembra* concert money on the proof offered by RBPI. RBPI has produced no evidence showing that Morgalo was a party to any of the relevant contracts. RBPI has produced no evidence showing that Morgalo acted as an agent of Blades or RBPI." The judge went as far as stating that "RBPI has pointed to no evidence that Morgalo and MM&A manipulated or used the corporate form to his detriment."[6]

Finally, I was vindicated. What I had been saying all this time was affirmed by the court. Rubén had had almost eight years to gather up all of the evidence he needed. But at the end of the day, all he had were accusations based on the testimony of people who had their own interests in mind, who were riding on the coattails of Rubén Blades. There was no evidence. No document. No smoking gun—only the allegations made by Ariel Rivas and Arturo Martinez. Yet Rubén Blades felt that his evidence was sufficient to prosecute to the fullest a case against me and attack me publicly, while at the same time not holding anyone else accountable.

The decision by the court was final. There was no more case against me. However, there was one more matter to dispense with, and that was the status of my pending appeal for the defamation case.

25

APPEALS COURT VICTORY

THE YEAR **2012** STARTED out even better than 2011. I had won all of my court battles and was still standing toe-to-toe against Rubén Blades and his team of lawyers. I put out another press release, and once again it was well received by the media. I finally had a voice. Although the media, particularly in Puerto Rico, still seemed to lean more to Rubén Blades' side, they did report the news. It was a good feeling to counter those news articles that had painted me as a thief for so long with the truth.

Then on February 27, 2012, the First Circuit Court of Appeals finally made a decision on my defamation case. It had been almost three years since it was dismissed. The appeals court formally rejected the conclusion made by Judge Justo Arenas in deciding to dismiss my defamation case. The court stated, "Because we disagree with that conclusion, as a matter of law, we find that the dismissal on that basis, and weighing all of the relevant factors, was an abuse of discretion."[1]

This was a huge issue in the press. The judge had abused his discretion! This was covered all over the news, particularly in Puerto Rico, and it was not good for Rubén Blades. He had a scheduled concert in Puerto Rico coming up in the beginning of April with Juan Luis Guerra and Draco Rosa. It was a highly anticipated, media-covered concert event, and the press was sure to be there. There was no way Rubén could avoid the publicity. I held off on my press release to coincide with his arrival in Puerto Rico. So the week before his concert, we released the court's ruling to the press.

Before Rubén Blades arrived in Puerto Rico, I was given an interview with Javier Ceriani from a popular television show called *Paparazzi Magazine*. He was a true professional. He treated me with respect, asked me relevant questions, and most importantly, took the time to verify what I was saying. He also gave Rubén Blades the opportunity to respond.

Shortly after my television interview, we found out through the discovery process that Arturo Martinez was traveling with Juan Toro and Rubén Blades for that show in Puerto Rico. When Javier Ceriani caught up with Rubén Blades at the hotel with a camera crew, he asked him if Arturo worked with him and if Arturo was there with him. Rubén emphatically denied it and then turned the conversation toward me saying, "Let's see if he shows up for trial." Then he looked into the camera and said in Spanish, "Aparecete" or "Show up."[2] He was visibly upset, and his statement implied that somehow I wouldn't show up. I was the one suing him for defamation, the one that wanted to clear my name. Why wouldn't I show up?

Interestingly enough, although Rubén Blades denied that Arturo worked with him or traveled with him on his shows, Arturo Martinez' Facebook posting showed something entirely different.[3] In fact, his postings regarding that show in Puerto Rico went like this, "It's on! On my way to the Juan Luis Guerra, Robi Draco Rosa & Rubén Blades concert in PR at the Coliseo. 1st of 2 shows sold out! at Sheraton Hotel, Puerto Rico Convention Center, San Juan, PR." Then, "My favorite part of touring. In about ½ hour 14000 seats will be full. SOLD OUT!" Then, "Damn, I love my job! With Rubén Blades, and 2 others at Coliseo de Puerto Rico." So it was clear that Arturo was there in Puerto Rico in the same hotel and the same show as Rubén Blades, stating that he loved his job with Rubén Blades, and it was his favorite part of touring. But Rubén claimed no knowledge and even denied it.

At a press conference for that show, the press asked Rubén about the appeals court decision. He replied in detail that he was happy that this was finally going to be done and that he was looking forward to it. He was sitting next to Juan Luis Guerra and Draco Rosa, and I would imagine it had to be somewhat embarrassing for him. I was saddened and conflicted by what I was witnessing. I never wanted it to go this far. All of this could have been avoided if we could have just sat down when I sent him those letters back in 2008. Four years had passed, and many decisions had been made by both of us that ultimately resulted in this spectacle. I didn't want to hurt Rubén, but he was unwilling to accept that I had no involvement. At this point, we were both too far into it to do anything other than ride it out to the end.

26

MEDIATION

ONCE THE DEFAMATION CASE was sent back to the District
Court of Puerto Rico for trial, it was like a huge weight
was lifted off my shoulders. All these years of carrying the
scorn and humiliation that came with being accused of something
I had not done had finally come to an end. I was no longer on the
defensive, trying to prove I hadn't done anything wrong. The court's
rulings had already given me all the vindication I needed, except for
this: as I mentioned at the beginning of this book, I'd never wanted
to sue Rubén. I just wanted him to hear my side. I just wanted him
to look in my eyes and realize that I never took anything from him
and that what he was told about me was not true. Even if the entire

world could somehow now realize that I was right, it would mean nothing if Rubén still didn't believe it.

Shortly before the day of the trial, the judge ordered us to try to reach an amicable resolution. I was willing to move forward with a resolution that would allow us to put this whole thing behind us and allow Rubén the opportunity to avoid a trial. There were several offers going back and forth between our attorneys and real opportunities for resolution, but I was the only one making any concessions. It became clear that Rubén had no interest in accepting the truth.

I've tried to put myself in his shoes many times to try to understand why he was so unwilling to be reasonable or face the facts. It became obvious to me that to do so would mean that the very foundation of his relationship with Ariel Rivas was established upon a pretense. Ever since the 2003 *Siembra* concert, Ariel Rivas had developed a close working relationship with Rubén that was both personally and commercially successful. They had collaborated on many tours and concerts around the world, produced and coproduced records, and had won Grammy awards for their collaboration. To accept the truth that I was presenting would have upended the last nine years of his professional life.

Since we were unable to reach an agreement in advance of the trial, Judge Bruce J. McGiverin ordered us to meet in his chambers on the Friday before the trial date. He called upon the now-retired Judge Justo Arenas, to mediate for us in order to try to resolve the matter before trial, which would be held on Monday, February 11, 2013. I flew down to Puerto Rico two days before our mediation. My brother flew down with me. He had been my biggest supporter and source of encouragement from the beginning of this whole ordeal. Every time I felt discouraged or beaten, he was always there by my side to remind me that I was not alone and that, no matter what challenges came my way, no matter how impossible the odds seemed, as long as I fought for the truth, then everything would be okay regardless of the outcome.

The night before the scheduled mediation, I was both anxious and resolved. I was anxious to get this ordeal settled and resolved to take it all the way. I was hopeful that by sitting down with Rubén just once more as we had done back in 2009 at his deposition, he would be reasonable and he would admit that he knew I had nothing to do with what he was accusing me of. I was ready to drop the case altogether if he would just admit that I hadn't stolen from him. I didn't want his money. I didn't want a single penny from him. I just wanted closure.

But that closure would not come on that day. I showed up early as usual to the conference room with my attorneys for mediation. Judge Justo Arenas and Pamela Gonzalez were also there. To my surprise, Rubén Blades was a no-show. I was upset. I was there, ready and willing to sit down and resolve this matter. I was willing to walk away, but he didn't even have the decency or courtesy to show up. Judge Arenas asked us to try to reach a settlement anyway. But the conversations were not very productive. Not because we couldn't have reached a reasonable solution, but because I was negotiating with Rubén's attorney, not with Rubén directly. She assured me that Rubén would be willing to make public statements that I hadn't done anything wrong. But when I asked why he was not there, Pamela responded that he could be called on the phone if needed. I found that to be very disrespectful. He was willing to accuse me publicly, but he was unwilling to face me or confront me privately. In contrast, I was the accused, and I had no problem facing my accuser. I was there, but where was he?

After several hours of attempting to find a resolution and not reaching one, Judge Justo Arenas suggested that we call Rubén Blades and that both Rubén and I could speak to each other. This was an opportunity that I did not take. I was angry that Rubén was not there and that he was unwilling to face me. I thought that the time for telephone conversations was long past. His not being physically present was a demonstration of his unwillingness to face the truth.

But I was also afraid. I felt that if I did speak to Rubén over the phone, he would ask me to forgive him, and I would have. Not taking the opportunity to speak with Rubén on that day is a decision that I immensely regret. In hindsight, I truly believe that if I had taken that opportunity, then Rubén would have finally realized I was telling him the truth. But his decision not to be present at the meeting was the sole contributing factor for my not agreeing to speak with him over the phone. I declined, and the mediation was over.

It was Friday, and the trial would begin on Monday.

27

MY DAY IN COURT

FEBRUARY 11, 2013, THE date of the defamation trial against Rubén Blades, finally came. It had been five long and personally aggravating years for me. The anger, humiliation, pain, and grief that consumed me all those years as the result of Rubén Blades' careless and accusatory statements made in the press—as well as the relentless and almost never ending legal tactics and maneuvers—were now at the verge of justice. What that justice would look like was still unknown. But I was certain that just having my day in court would be justice enough for me. It wasn't about winning or losing. It was about demonstrating my character and integrity through my presence and perseverance.

The night before the trial, my brother and I were staying at a friend's house in Puerto Rico, and we were both praying and meditating over the case. I did not want to hurt Rubén, but I wanted him to admit that I was not at fault. I didn't want to shake up his life or try to get back anything I'd lost. I was resolved that the past was the past and the future was what we needed to focus on. My brother suggested to me that we should call Rubén Blades to the stand first, and if he acknowledged that I hadn't done anything wrong, we could rest the case. I was in agreement because I was thinking the same thing, but I decided I would ask my attorneys and get their advice.

The morning of the trial, we met at my attorneys' office first. To my surprise they both suggested the same thing my brother and I had discussed before we even had a chance to bring it up. To me, it was confirmation that this was the right thing to do. So we went into court ready to present our case with all of the evidence and documents to support our claims.

When we arrived at court, there was very little media. I was surprised at this, since every time Rubén had been there in the past, there was a host of media coverage. The only press I saw was Javier Ceriani from *Paparazzi TV*, someone from an Internet blog, and a familiar face from *Primera Hora*, a newspaper from Puerto Rico that had covered this case since the beginning and, in my view, had served more as a platform for Rubén's statements than as a news publication.

On my side of the courtroom were my attorneys, Juan Frontera and Israel Alicea. We were seated on the left side of the courtroom with the media seated directly behind us. I was at the far left of the table with my attorneys. On the right side of the courtroom was Pamela Gonzalez along with her co-counsel Eduardo J. Corretjer-Reyes. Sitting at their table was Rubén Blades. Behind them were Rubén's witnesses, Arturo Martinez, Ariel Rivas, and Juan Toro.

The bailiff announced, "All rise! The Honorable Bruce J. McGiverin presiding." And with that the trial began.

There were a few administrative matters that were still pending before the court that needed be resolved. These matters included some inclusions of evidence and minor stipulations or agreements amongst the parties. Once those matters were addressed by the court, we were ready for the witnesses.

I would like to bring your attention to the witness list before we go any further. This is important, because our decision to not call me to the witness stand would later come back as an allegation by Rubén Blades' camp that I "refused" to take the stand. For my witness list, we had only two names: Ruben Blades and Robert Morgalo. Rubén Blades' witness list included Ruben Blades, Arturo Martinez, Ariel Rivas, Juan Toro, *and* Robert Morgalo. So they could have called me to the stand at any time.

Our case against Rubén Blades was a pretty straightforward defamation case. We argued that Rubén Blades had made statements to third parties (the media) and that those statements were false when he accused me of a crime and, therefore, caused me damages. All of those elements are needed to prove defamation. So our strategy was very simple: call Rubén Blades to the stand and ask him about those statements and what his frame of mind was when he said them. If Rubén's statements were consistent with our claims against him— that he had made those statement and that he had accused me of stealing money—then we would rest our case.

On the flip side of our claim against Rubén was his defense. And he threw in everything but the kitchen sink to defend himself. He argued that his statements were hyperbole or exaggerations, while also claiming they were factual. He made many claims that his statements were made in reference only to the company, Martinez, Morgalo & Associates, and never toward me personally. However, the evidence that we presented showed a consistent pattern of Rubén accusing me of stealing, embezzling, committing larcenous acts, and misappropriating funds. For example, we presented a letter written by Rubén Blades to Willie Colón, dated May 14, 2003—just eleven days after the *Siembra* concert and while I was still in Iraq (see Appendix K). In the letter Rubén wrote, "I also want to clarify the extent of Roberto Morgalo's involvement in this situation. So far, Arturo is the one we all have focused on, but it seems to me it's obvious Morgalo had a hand as well in the embezzlement, and it's in Arturo's personal interest to explain what role the latter played in this." He went on to state in this letter that, "I regret this whole situation, and I am trying to clarify it and to resolve it ASAP. Please, be patient. As for Arturo and Morgalo, the only reason I have waited before going through with criminal action against them is that we need to understand what was the final amount stolen." It is evident that Blades was accusing me of embezzling and stealing money. Not the company, as he was testifying in court in his defense, but me individually. How could he say he'd never accused me personally in light of this evidence? And this was not the only evidence we confronted him with at trial.

When confronted with the statements he'd made at the press conference in Panama, Rubén denied making any accusation against me or Arturo. He claimed that he'd only spoken about the company. He was asked under oath, "So, you never identified, during that press conference, the specific names of Arturo Martinez and Robert Morgalo?" Rubén's answer was, "Correct."[1] Then my attorney presented Exhibits 1 and 2 to the court to be entered as evidence and confronted Rubén with these. They were news articles dated May 9, 2007, and one of them entitled, "*Blades Apendado con Demanda de Colón*" or "Blades Saddened by Colón's Claims," was carried through the Associated Press. The article stated as follows: "The representative, with whom, according to Blades, he had worked without problems for several years, were identified as Arturo Martinez and Robert Morgalo." It went on to say, "He didn't sue his two representatives because they didn't have money."[2] Once again, Rubén was on the stand under oath, denying that he made those statements about me individually.

As another line of defense, Rubén moved from asserting facts as a defense to hiding behind opinions. When asked by my attorney, "The fact is, Mr. Blades, that you have stated to Mr. Morgalo specifically that you think that he stole from you and embezzled you. Is that right?" Rubén's response was not very convincing, "If I told…if I said that, which I don't remember, I'm sure I said it because that's what I…that's my opinion." This line of questioning continued on for a short while. Finally, my attorney asked this, "When you made the statement in the press conference, in Panama…you believed that he had stolen money from [you] and embezzled you, is that correct?" Rubén's answer: "I believed that they were both involved, yes." My attorney then said, "I have no further questions, Your Honor."[3]

My attorney looked at me, and I was completely satisfied. I nodded my head in approval. Although Rubén had tried every way possible to squirm his way out of admitting that he had accused me personally of anything—that he was talking about the company, that it was hyperbole, that it was opinion—the evidence was just too much. He had no choice but to acknowledge what he had said and that he'd said it about me as an individual and not about the company. Since we had gotten what we needed from Rubén Blades' testimony under oath and supported it with the evidence, we rested our case. I didn't have any need to go on the stand because I was prosecuting the case, and we had already proved it.

28

PARADE OF WITNESSES

Now it was Rubén Blades' attorneys' time to present their defense. As I mentioned before, they had five witnesses on their list, including me. They could have called me to the stand at any time to examine me—to barrage me with questions, to dissect every piece of evidence, to discredit me, to impeach my testimony—but they didn't. Yet after this, they stated in a press release that I had "refused" to take the stand. Furthermore, I had previously taken the stand on my own accord at the default hearing, not to mention that Rubén Blades' attorney had already taken my deposition.

Why didn't they call me? My guess is, they already had my testimony from that previous deposition and from the default hearing, and they knew it would not serve them well for me to repeat my testimony in court. Instead, they called their other witnesses.

Just as before at the default hearing, Pamela Gonzalez paraded her witnesses and coddled them with softball and leading questions. "Isn't it true *this*," or "isn't it true *that*." Their testimonies were uneventful with nothing new to present. We already had their previous testimonies from their depositions and the default hearing, as well as all of the documented evidence we had discovered throughout the process. There was one big difference, however. Unlike the one-sided arguments at the default hearing three years earlier, this time their testimony was challenged. It was put to the test through cross-examination and scrutinized against their previous testimony and confronted with evidence.

First up was Ariel Rivas. Of the many questions Rubén's attorney asked, several stand out as worth commenting on. First, "Who did you negotiate the *Siembra* concert with?" His answer: "With Robert Morgalo."[1] As you already know, the evidence did not support this statement. Ariel's letter to Arturo Martinez, dated January 20, 2003, irrefutably showed that he had negotiated the terms of the contract with Arturo Martinez. Furthermore, all of the contracts, e-mails, and confirmation letters had been sent from Arturo Martinez, and none of them ever included my name. There was no proof whatsoever of any connection between those negotiations and me.

Ariel Rivas kept insisting that I had negotiated those contracts with him. However, when pressed by my attorney upon cross-examination, he could not even identify which of the three versions of the contact was the one that was actually signed. In fact, no signed contract has ever been produced as evidence. When my attorney asked which contract was allegedly signed by him, he stated, "I can tell you that I am sure as to the one that was not signed."[2] Then he points to one of the three contracts. As it turns out, the one he identified and testified under oath as not being signed is precisely the one he had presented in his previous deposition as the one he *did* sign. What's more, he is the one who, according to his own testimony, printed it up and introduced it as evidence. Now at trial, he emphatically stated that it was not the one he signed.

The most memorable thing about Ariel Rivas' testimony was that he was noticeably uncomfortable and fidgeting. He bounced back and forth with his statements, apparently trying hard to be as evasive as possible. A simple question such as, "You don't have any document to establish that you had negotiated that with Mr. Robert Morgalo in December. Is that right?" was met with, "I would have to check all my e-mails."[3] Five years of litigation and sitting on the witness stand, and he still had to check his e-mails? He had no evidence to support his allegations. All he had was his own testimony that was discredited throughout his cross-examination.

When asked by my attorney, "Now, do you have any document, Mr. Rivas, to establish that you transferred sixty-two thousand, five hundred dollars to Martinez & Morgalo Associates, in April 2002, for the Cheo Feliciano and Rubén Blades concert?" The response and subsequent exchange went like this:

> Ariel Rivas: I must have some confirmation, yes.
>
> Frontera-Suau: I'm asking you do you have it?
>
> Ariel Rivas: I must have some confirmation, yes.
>
> Frontera-Suau: The truth is that you don't have any type of documentary evidence that you, in fact, transferred those sixty-two thousand, five hundred dollars, in April 2002.
>
> Ariel Rivas: We must have the bank register.

> Frontera-Suau: And, the fact is that you don't have any document where it is stated that the alleged payment of sixty-two thousand, five hundred dollars...was applied to the *Siembra* Concert.
>
> Ariel Rivas: Of course I do, the contract.
>
> Frontera-Suau: The one that you don't have here?
>
> Ariel Rivas: The one I don't have here.[4]

It was painful to watch but at the same time compelling. He was way out of his league. I could not understand how Rubén could watch this taking place and not question Ariel's judgment. Ariel Rivas is a graduate from Berkley and has been working with Rubén Blades since 2003. Yet, he could not produce a single document supporting his allegations, and when challenged, he resorted to answers such as, "I would have to check my e-mails."

29

BOMBSHELLS

EXT UP, ARTURO MARTINEZ. Just as with Ariel Rivas, the questions asked by Rubén Blades' attorney were generic and not new to the discussion. Everything previously testified was regurgitated on the witness stand, with some exceptions. One question in particular that Pamela Gonzalez asked was, "Do you know if he [Robert Morgalo] had access to the accounts remotely from wherever he was, to the Martinez and Morgalo...bank accounts?" Arturo's response was, "Yes. He also had a bank card."[1] This statement was stunning for two reasons. One, that I would have had access to an ATM while in combat in Iraq was ludicrous, and two, the statement completely contradicted his own testimony at the default hearing. Of course, there was no cross-examination in that hearing. At this trial, there would be. My attorney went straight to the point with his first line of questioning. It went like this:

> Frontera-Suau: Now, you testified that Mr. Robert Morgalo, after he was deployed to military services, had access to the accounts. Is that right?
>
> Arturo: Yes.
>
> Frontera-Suau: Do you remember giving testimony here, in the Default Hearings against Martinez & Morgalo, Mr. Martinez?
>
> Arturo: Yeah.
>
> Frontera-Suau: Do you remember testifying, during those hearings, that Mr. Robert Morgalo had no access to the accounts of the corporation?
>
> Arturo: No, I don't.
>
> Frontera-Suau: No. I am going to show you page one-eighty-two of the Default Hearings.... Lines six to nine, and I am going to read it to you. You stated there: "Again, I don't remember, but, if they were sent, I would have sent them.... If they were sent, because Robert was away, so he had no access to that, to the accounts, and sending any money."
>
> Frontera-Suau: That was your testimony at the Default Hearings. Is that right?
>
> Arturo: Uh huh, yes.[2]

It felt like a "gotcha" moment, but with all of the bombshell testimony to come, it was of minor consequence to find him contradicting his own testimony.

Going back to Pamela Gonzalez' questioning of Arturo Martinez, one particular line of questioning shocked the media in the courtroom. It was Arturo's testimony regarding his incarceration.

I was surprised that Rubén's attorney even brought it up. I didn't think it was relevant to the defamation case and could potentially be damaging to Rubén Blades with respect to his judgment and to his knowledge of the crime of which Arturo was convicted.

The questions went like this:

> Gonzalez: Mr. Martinez, you were incarcerated in 2003, correct?
>
> Arturo: August 22, 2003.
>
> Gonzalez: And, can you tell the Court what that offense was?
>
> Arturo: Yes, I was convicted, in the State of Georgia, for trafficking drugs.
>
> Gonzalez: What were the circumstances of that offense? What were you specifically charged with?
>
> Arturo: My charge was trafficking cocaine. I was sentenced to fifteen years in the State of Georgia. I was bringing in half a 'kilo' of cocaine....
>
> Gonzalez: From where?
>
> Arturo: From Panama. I was attempting to win my name back...win money back to try and pay back the tremendous debt.
>
> Gonzalez: To Mr. Blades?
>
> Arturo: To Mr. Blades, to Mr. Colón, to people from the radio stations, to anyone I could... desperation. I'm not condoning it at all or even excusing myself, but I was just trying to do something.[3]

The reaction from the media was priceless. The one reporter from *Primera Hora* who had been following the case and shown up at all the proceedings, sat there with her jaw dropped open. She was looking around to see if anyone else was hearing the same thing. I looked at her and nodded my head as confirmation of what was being said on the witness stand. Her shock was unmistakable. Here was Rubén Blades' star witness testifying that he had gone to Panama, of all places, to get cocaine to sell so that he could give the money to Rubén Blades.

But even this was not the most jaw-dropping development during Arturo's testimony. As the questioning progressed, it was determined that Arturo Martinez had been released from prison after serving five years of his fifteen-year sentence. It was also determined that upon his release, he started working immediately for Juan Toro at The Relentless Agency—Rubén Blades' own representing agency.

When asked his position at the agency, he responded with, "I do work in bookings, I do road work."

"You're an agent?" asked Pamela Gonzalez.

"Yes," replied Arturo.[4]

Imagine that. Arturo gets out of prison for trying to sell cocaine to pay money owed to Rubén Blades, and then he goes to work right away for Rubén Blades' agent.

But wait. There's more.

When it was my attorney's turn to cross-examine Arturo, we presented evidence as to the nature of his employment with Rubén Blades' agent, Juan Toro.

In order for you to better appreciate this fact, I would like to put it into context. If you recall, while I was still acting as my own lawyer, the judge in Puerto Rico allowed the attorneys to go to the prison where Arturo was incarcerated in order to take his deposition. When I finally got my hands on that deposition, I was mystified by what I was reading. I could not understand why Arturo was making the statements he had. So when I was able to hire my own attorneys, I asked them to subpoena Arturo's prison records. There we discovered that, just around the time of the deposition, Juan Toro went to visit Arturo in prison. On the visitation card, he listed himself as Arturo's employer. Imagine that! Rubén Blades' agent goes to visit a witness in the case—and this is not disclosed to anyone—and he is listed as Arturo's employer.

We presented this evidence at trial, and it did not look good for Rubén. This was a man who had run for the presidency of Panama—a man who has recently stated he wants to run a second time in the 2019 election! What does all this say about his judgment, his dealings, his associations? I am not accusing anyone of anything. In fact, I don't think Rubén put these puzzle pieces together before this. But what in the world was going on here?

Another one of those revealing moments came when it was discovered that on or around the 2003 *Siembra* concert, and right around the time of Arturo's suicide attempt, Arturo gave Juan Toro access to the company bank accounts. The testimony at trial went like this:

> Frontera-Suau: Now, you gave access, to Mr. Juan Toro, to the account of Martinez & Morgalo Associates right before or after the concert of May 3, 2003. Is that right?
>
> Arturo: Correct.
>
> Frontera-Suau: And, at that point, you didn't know how much money was in the Martinez, & Morgalo Associates' account. Is that right?
>
> Arturo: Correct.
>
> Frontera-Suau: So you didn't know... you don't know how much money Juan Toro took out at that point in time. Is that right?
>
> Arturo: Correct....
>
> Frontera-Suau: Why did you give Juan Toro access to the Martinez & Morgalo account, after the *Siembra* show?
>
> Arturo: I was hospitalized. I was told that Rubén needed anything that was there already....
>
> Frontera-Suau: So, what information did you give Juan Toro?

> Arturo: I gave him the bank code.
>
> Frontera-Suau: So that he could withdraw the money to give to Rubén Blades?
>
> Arturo: Correct.[5]

Now, stop and think about that for a minute. I was deployed to Iraq and had no access to the bank accounts or any knowledge of what was going on. Yet, Arturo Martinez gave access to our company bank accounts to Juan Toro, who is now both his employer and Rubén Blades' agent. Also particularly interesting: When Juan Toro was called to the witness stand and asked when he had started his company, The Relentless Agency, he answered, "The actual agency was formed in 2003."[6,7] And on top of that, no one—not Arturo Martinez, Juan Toro, or Rubén Blades—seemed to know just how much money was in the Martinez & Morgalo bank account at the time.

Juan Toro's testimony after that was relatively unremarkable, except that it shed some light as to his relationship with Ariel Rivas, Arturo Martinez, and Rubén Blades. He testified that he didn't know much about the inner workings of the *Siembra* show or of Rubén Blades' defamatory statements. So as he completed his testimony, the case came to a close.

What was apparent after all of this is that all of the parties involved directly with the *Siembra* show and its funds were now all working with or for Rubén Blades, and all were now testifying on his behalf. They presented no evidence against me except their testimony, which was discredited and contradicted by their own previous testimonies and by actual hard evidence.

As we walked out of the courtroom, I saw Juan Toro, Ariel Rivas, and Arturo Martinez standing by the elevator. I approached Juan to say hello. Ariel quickly stepped away, leaving just Juan and

Arturo. My conversation with Juan was cordial. I told him he looked good and exchanged minor pleasantries. I looked at Arturo who was standing to my right, and he was practically fuming. I looked him in the eye and could tell he was extremely agitated. I, however, was at peace. I thought about saying something to Arturo, but I could tell there was nothing to say. They got into the elevator and left the building.

As I left with my lawyers and my brother, I felt extremely satisfied with the trial and how the truth had played out. I knew that no matter what the judge decided, I would accept it. There was nothing further I could do to change the minds and perceptions that people have had about me. But now I had everyone on the record. They could spin the outcome anyway they wanted, but their own testimonies and the evidence were now public record. And that record speaks for itself.

30

AT THE END OF THE DAY

SOON AFTER THE TRIAL, the judge dismissed my defamation claim against Rubén Blades. He ruled that although I had proved defamation, there was substantial truth in the statements made by Rubén Blades, because Arturo himself had testified that he had mismanaged the funds.[1]

The judge's opinion was a scathing rebuke of my defamation case. Although I was resolved to accept whatever the outcome, his decision took me by surprise. I had felt that we had accomplished what we set out to do—to hold Rubén accountable for his statements. But I was so focused on Rubén's testimony and statements to the press, that I failed to see that by not calling myself as a witness, I created an opening for him.

It was like a badly played chess move, focusing on the king while ignoring the pawns. Once again, Rubén had the advantage of an uncontested defense, similar to what had happened in the default hearing. Although we had the opportunity to cross-examine Rubén's witnesses here, the fact remains that we provided them with undisputed testimony by not calling me to the stand. As the Honorable Judge McGiverin stated, "And since Morgalo neither introduced any written contract nor put on conflicting testimony (such as his own), I find Rivas' version to be more likely true than not."[2]

My decision to not take the stand and to leave it up to Rubén Blades' attorney to call me to it proved fatal to my case. I had handed Rubén his victory. The only testimonies at trial, even though they were plagued with contradictions, were those of Rubén and his witnesses. There was no testimony for the judge to hear to counter theirs. Because of this, the court took everything that was stated by Arturo and Ariel as undisputed facts.

I don't blame the judge here. In fact, I understand his decision, and as devastating as it was to hear, it was fair and just according to the law. He could only base his decision on what was presented in court. And on that day—the day for which I had waited so long—I fell short.

Still, at the end of the day, no one had produced any evidence connecting me with the *Siembra* contract or showing that I had been involved in anyway. That should have been the end of that. But it was not.

True to form, Rubén Blades took the opportunity to stoke the fire again. This time, he sent out a press release in English and Spanish, with the words well crafted. Although there was no inaccuracy in his statements, they were put together in a manner that still depicted me as having had something to do with those events. He even went so far as to state, "Morgalo refused to testify."[3] Remember, he'd had every opportunity to call me to the witness stand, but he did not.

The fact that Rubén deemed it necessary to continue mischaracterizing my involvement and portray me in a manner that somehow places responsibility upon me for what happened demonstrated a poor assessment of the facts and evidence bordering on the delusional. It seemed to me that Rubén was fighting for his pride and public image more than anything else.

But to me, the truth was worth fighting for, no matter the odds, no matter the outcome.

31

THE ROAD BEST TRAVELED

IN COMBAT, ONE WITNESSES the ravages of war. The battle lines are not always clearly drawn, but the landscape is recognizable. There are good guys and bad guys and those caught up and displaced by the mess. Collateral damage comes with the business of war. It is inevitable. But collateral damage is not limited to the confines of the battlefield. It can bear heavy on those far removed from the action, and wound just as much. I really can't blame anyone for their decisions or even their actions as they pertain to this story. They were all in some form or fashion a part of the collateral damage that comes with war. The series of events that took place following the attacks of 9/11 ultimately led to another series of events that culminated in this story's outcome. I make no apologies for serving my country. I would do it again if called to do so. But it is unfortunate that so many people I cared about were so deeply affected by my deployment.

Arturo is without a doubt the biggest casualty in this story. He was handed a raw deal that he hadn't signed up for. He lost five years of his life because he found himself in a situation that he couldn't get out of. Unlike me, he did not have battle buddies to watch his back. No one was there in the fight with him. He was alone and facing unimaginable pressure. He almost took his own life and ultimately made some very bad decisions as a direct result of my being deployed. I hold myself responsible for him. I failed him. I failed to properly pass the responsibilities of the company over to him. While I had only five days to deploy, I had previously had three years to build him up as an executive of the company. If I had known then what I know now, I would have been a better leader, and things would have been different.

It is regrettable that Rubén Blades and Willie Colón ended up as hostile combatants in such a public and embarrassing dispute. In the eyes of the fans and the general public, what was once a dynamic duo that personified salsa music was now relegated to a dirty battle over money. The legacy and the image of these two icons has been forever tarnished by their own battle scars. The cold yet cordial relationship they had maintained over the years may have been irreparably severed. But the state of their relationship is not my responsibility. There is no doubt in my mind that if I had not deployed, things would have turned out differently. But I was not a party to their internal discussions or alleged agreement with respect to the *Siembra* concert. That was between these two men. Nor am I responsible for their decisions to ignore the situation or file lawsuits against each other or even fail to find a middle ground.

Looking back, there are many things that I could have done differently that might have changed the course of their actions. Perhaps I could have done a better job in demonstrating my character and integrity to Rubén. If after four years of working together, he didn't know who I was, then perhaps I had failed to show him.

Willie Colón never once accused me of anything. For this I am grateful. He presented himself at all times as a true gentleman and professional. I regret that he had to go through such an ordeal. Given the fact that his full involvement with this case was that of an artist performing a reunion concert—a concert where he was not paid his full amount—I do not blame him. His actions and his decisions, as far as I could see, were tempered and reasonable given the circumstances.

As for Ariel Rivas, I will give him the benefit of the doubt because I truly do not know him. I cannot speak for him, nor do I know what he was going through. His decisions and actions were his to make, and he is responsible for them.

By the grace of God, I have lived and experienced an incredibly full life. My journey has taken me from humble beginnings to places I would never have imagined I'd go. The values my mother and grandmother instilled in me as a young boy have served me well. I honor them, not just with words but also with my actions, by how I have lived my life, and how I have conducted myself. I have fought the good fight and never backed down. I have raised myself up every time I have fallen. I have taken bold chances, without fear or reservations, knowing that I can do anything as long as I am willing to work for it and never give up. I am who I am—nothing more and nothing less. I may not have a lot, but what I do have is more than enough.

I am retired now from both the military and the music business. The most important thing for me at this point is to take everything that I have learned—the good and the bad, the struggles and the successes—and use them to set an example for my children. To let them know that life is not always fair. That justice comes in many forms. That sometimes, the road less traveled is the road best traveled. That struggles make you stronger. That forgiveness sets you free. That truth is never compromised. And that nothing is impossible if it's important enough to you.

As for that penny? I still have it, tucked away in my wallet as a reminder that honor and dignity are more valuable than riches. It is a reminder of my journey and of my perseverance and resilience. It is a reminder of the truth. And it is in that truth that I find serenity and closure.

APPENDIX A

Contract for Rubén Blades
2002 Concert

Deposit Received	Date Received

MARTINEZ, MORGALO & ASSOCIATES
64 FULTON ST. SUITE 601
NEW YORK, NY 10038
TEL. 212 349-4001
FAX 212 349-4002
E-MAIL. MARTINEZMORGALO@aol.com

ENGAGEMENT CONTRACT

THIS CONTRACT is for the personal services of artist on the engagement described below made this 30ᵀᴴ day of **MAY 2002** between the undersigned Purchaser of Music, (herein called Purchaser) and Artist.

1) Name of Artist: **RUBEN BLADES**
featuring Editus Ensemble

2) Billing Agreement: **100% SOLE TOP BILLING ON ALL FORMS OF ADVERTISING AND PROMOTIONS**

3) Name and Address of Place of Engagement: **COLISEO ROBERTO CLEMENTE HATO REY, PUERTO RICO**

4) Date, Starting and Finishing time of engagement: **SATURDAY DECEMBER 7, 2002 ONE 90 MINUTE SET. STARTING TIME :TBA**

5) Type of engagement: **CONCERT**

6) Wage agreed upon: **$ 125,000.00 U.S. DOLLARS PLUS AIRFARES,HOTEL, GROUND,SOUND, LIGHTS AND ALL RIDER REQUIREMENTS.**

7) Employer will make payment as follows: **DEPOSIT IN THE AMOUNT OF $62,500.00 U.S. DUE NO LATER THAN JUNE 7, 2002 IN WIRE TRANSFER, CASH, CERTIFIED CHECK OR MONEY ORDER PAYABLE TO MARTINEZ, MORGALO & ASSOCIATES, INC. BALANCE OF $62,500.00 U.S. DOLLARS DUE NO LATER THAN NOVEMBER 7, 2002 IN WIRE TRANSFER,CASH, CERTIFIED CHECK OR MONEY ORDER PAYABLE TO MARTINEZ, MORGALO & ASSOCIATES, INC. FULL PAYMENT MUST BE RECEIVED BY NOVEMBER 7, 2002 BY MARTINEZ MORGALO & ASSOCIATES INC.**

7a) The above form and method of payment are understood to be of the essence of this agreement. The ARTIST shall not perform if ARTIST has not received any and all outstanding compensation, balances or moneys prior to start of performance. In the event that payments are not made as herein provided, ARTIST shall at its option, have the right to refuse to perform and PURCHASER shall remain liable to ARTIST for the agreed price herein set forth.

07-13ᴿ
DEPOSITION
EXHIBIT 2

MARTINEZ, MORGALO and ASSOCIATES
350 BROADWAY • SUITE 1211 • NEW YORK CITY, NY 10013 • TEL. (212) 966-8499 • FAX. (212) 966-8599
martinezmorgalo@aol.com

ADDITIONAL TERMS AND CONDITIONS

MARTINEZ, MORGALO & ASSOCIATES. acts solely as an agent for Artist(s) herein and it is understood by purchaser that may in no way be held responsible for non-performance, lateness or any other action by Artist(s) which interfere with performance of this agreement.

Any musician hired to perform on this agreement is free to cease service hereunder by reason of any strike, ban, unfair list, order of requirement of Local 802 of the American Federation of Musicians. The agreement of the musicians to perform is further subject to proven inability due to sickness, accidents, or accidents by means of transportation, riots, strikes, epidemics, acts of God, or any other legitimate conditions beyond the control of the musicians.

In the event the employer fails, neglects or refuses to pay the wage or other payments agreed upon herein and suit is commenced to recover the aforesaid or any part thereof, the employer shall be responsible for the attorney's fees, court costs and expenses incurred in recovery of the sums due.

Purchaser shall pay and hold ARTIST harmless of and free of and from any and all taxes, fees, dues and the like to the engagement hereunder and the sums payable to the ARTIST shall be free of such taxes, fees, dues and the like.

ALL advertising and artwork is subject to the approval of
MARTINEZ, MORGALO & ASSOCIATES

NOTE: ANY CANCELLATION AFTER RAINOUT DATE BY PURCHASER WILL RESULT IN FORFEIT OF DEPOSIT.

**CESAR SAINZ FOR
ROMPEOLAS**

                               **MARTINEZ, MORGALO &
ASSOCIATES
F/S/O RUBEN BLADES**

_____

Print Employers Name   Print Leaders Name

_____

Signature of Employer   Signature of Leader

**CALLE HIJA DEL CARIBE # 208
HATO REY, PUERTO RICO**
Address   **ROBERTO MORGALO**
                                                Booking Agent

**787 747 3508 FAX
787 473 7777**
Telephone (Home & Business)

APPENDIX B

Wire Transfers to M&M from Promoter
for Rubén Blades' 2002 Concert

Client Support Unit
100 Citibank Drive
San Antonio, TX 78245

Ordered By:

ORDER PARTY:	CESAR SAINZ RODRIGUEZ URB LOS MAESTROS

Beneficiary:

BNF BNF:	A/C: 00283848 MARTINEZ MORGALO AND ASSOCIATES 350 BROADWAY STE 1211 NEW YORK NY 10013 3911

000001US0010001284 -000154000000-0001780627
MARTINEZ MORGALO AND ASSOCIATES
350 BROADWAY STE 1211
NEW YORK NY 10013 3911

DATE: JUNE 27, 2002
GID:
WC:
REL REF:
AMOUNT: USD*******$20,000.00
SAME DAY FUNDS

The credit to your account may have been
reduced by funds transfer charges of the
sending bank and/or Citibank.

Details of Payment:

DEBIT PARTY: BANCO POPULAR PR

Originator to beneficiary Information:
OBI: SEG DEP CONCIERTO RU
BEN BLADES PR 2 002

Bank to Bank Information:
BBK:

VALUE DATE: 06/27/02 **SAME DAY FUNDS** **AMOUNT**USD$20,000.00

CITIBANK⊕

Dear Customer,

This is to inform you that your account was credited with proceeds from a funds transfer payment.
Details are as follows:

Credit
Advice: MARTINEZ MORGALO AND ASSOCIATES
350 BROADWAY STE 1211
NEW YORK NY 10013 3911

Date: JUNE 27, 2002

Amount: USD*******$20,000.00

NON NEGOTIABLE

The Sum of: TWENTY THOUSAND AND 00/100 U.S. DOLLARS••

CREDIT ADVICE

Client Support Unit
100 Citibank Drive
San Antonio, TX 78245

Ordered By:

| ORDER PARTY: | CESAR SAINZ DBA ROMPEOLAS |
| | URB LOS MAESTROS |

Beneficiary:

BNF BNF:	A/C: 00283848
	MARTINEZ MORGALO AND ASSOCIATES
	64 FULTON STREET SUITE 601
	NEW YORK NY 10038

00000 1U50010001598 -000154000000 -0002781003
MARTINEZ MORGALO AND ASSOCIATES
64 FULTON STREET SUITE 601
NEW YORK NY 10038

DATE: OCTOBER 3, 2002
GID:
WC:
REL REF:
AMOUNT: USD********$20,000.00
SAME DAY FUNDS

The credit to your account may have been
reduced by funds transfer charges of the
sending bank and/or Citibank.

Details of Payment:

DEBIT PARTY: BANCO POPULAR PR

Originator to beneficiary Information:
OBI: 3ER DEP RUBEN BLADES
         23 NOV PR PAG ADO HASTA HOY
         USD52MIL

Bank to Bank Information:
BBK:

VALUE DATE: 10/03/02   SAME DAY FUNDS   **AMOUNT**USD$20,000.00

CITIBANK⊕

Dear Customer,

This is to inform you that your account was credited with proceeds from a funds transfer payment.
Details are as follows:

Credit
Advice: MARTINEZ MORGALO AND ASSOCIATES   Date: OCTOBER 3, 2002
            64 FULTON STREET SUITE 601
            NEW YORK NY 10038   Amount: USD********$20,000.00

NON NEGOTIABLE

The Sum of: TWENTY THOUSAND AND 00/100 U.S. DOLLARS•••

CREDIT ADVICE

Client Support Unit
100 Citibank Drive
San Antonio, TX 78245

Ordered By:

ORDER PARTY:	CESAR SAINZ URB LOS MAESTROS

Beneficiary:

BNF BNF:	A/C: 00283848 MARTINEZ MORGALO AND ASSOCIATES 64 FULTON STREET SUITE 601 NEW YORK NY 10038

00009IU50010002577 -000154000000-0003021029
MARTINEZ MORGALO AND ASSOCIATES
64 FULTON STREET SUITE 601
NEW YORK NY 10038

DATE: OCTOBER 29, 2002
GID:
WC:
REL REF:
AMOUNT: USD********$10,000.00
SAME DAY FUNDS

The credit to your account may have been
reduced by funds transfer charges of the
sending bank and/or Citibank.

Details of Payment:

DEBIT PARTY: BANCO POPULAR PR

Originator to beneficiary Information:
OBI: 3ER DEP RUBEN BLADES
            23 NOV PR PAGA DO HASTA HOY U
            SD62MIL

Bank to Bank Information:
BBK:

VALUE DATE: 10/29/02   **SAME DAY FUNDS**   **AMOUNT**USD$10,000.00

CITIBANK◆

Dear Customer,
This is to inform you that your account was credited with proceeds from a funds transfer payment.
Details are as follows:

		Date:	OCTOBER 29, 2002
Credit Advice:	MARTINEZ MORGALO AND ASSOCIATES 64 FULTON STREET SUITE 601 NEW YORK NY 10038	Amount:	USD********$10,000.00

NON NEGOTIABLE

The Sum of: TEN THOUSAND AND 00/100 U.S. DOLLARS••

CREDIT ADVICE

APPENDIX C

Wire Transfers from M&M to Rubén Blades Productions
for 2002 Rubén Blades' Concert

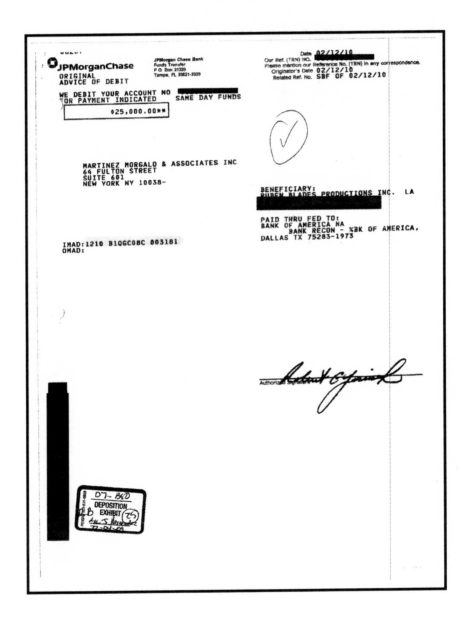

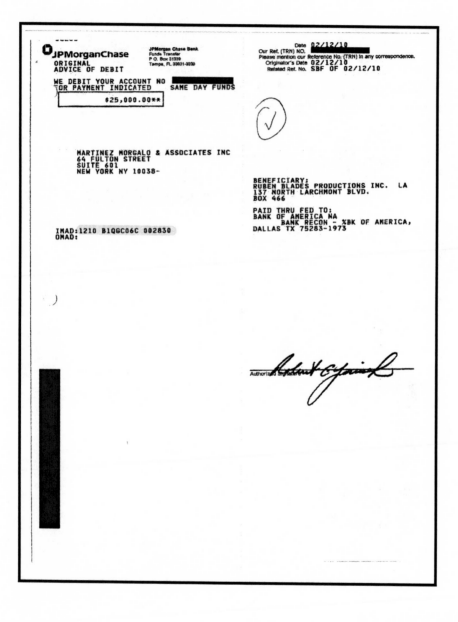

APPENDIX D

Siembra Contract

Version # 1

Deposit Received	Date Received

Martinez, Morgalo & Associates
64 Fulton Street
Suite 601
New York, NY 10038
TEL. 212 349-4001
FAX 212 349-4002
E-MAIL. Arturo@martinezmorgalo.com

ENGAGEMENT CONTRACT

THIS CONTRACT is for the personal services of artist on the engagement described below made this 22nd day of **January 2003** between the undersigned Purchaser of Music, (herein called employer) and artist.

1) Name of Artist: **RUBEN BLADES & WILLIE COLON**

2) Billing Agreement: 100% SOLE TOP BILLING ON ALL FORMS OF ADVERTISING AND PROMOTIONS

3) Name and Address of Place of Engagement:
**ESTADIO HIRAM BITHORN
SAN JUAN, PUERTO RICO**

4) Date, Starting and Finishing time of engagement:
**SATURDAY MAY 3RD, 2003
ONE CONCERT PERFORMANCE
OF MINIMUM 2 ½ HOURS
STARTING TIME AT TBD**

5) Type of engagement: CONCERT

6) Wage agreed upon:
$350,000.00 U.S. DOLLARS GUARANTEE, ALL- INCLUSIVE EXCEPT FOR SOUND & LIGHTS.

7) Employer will make payment as follows:
1ST DEPOSIT IN THE AMOUNT OF $62,500.00, U.S. DOLLARS DUE IMMEDIATELY.
2ND DEPOSIT IN THE AMOUNT OF $87,500.00 U.S. DOLLARS DUE MARCH 22nd 2003.
3RD DEPOSIT IN THE AMOUNT OF $87,500.00 U.S DOLLARS DUE APRIL 1st 2003.
BALANCE OF $112,500.00 U.S. DOLLARS SHALL BE PAID NO LATER THAN April 22nd 2003.

PAYMENTS MUST BE MADE IN THE FORM OF WIRE TRANFER, CASH, CERTIFIED CHECK OR MONEY ORDER PAYABLE TO MARTINEZ, MORGALO AND ASSOCIATES. (ARTIST MUST RECEIVE PAYMENT IN FULL 14 DAYS PRIOR TO DEPARTURE FOR PUERTO RICO)

EXHIBIT
1

0025

#YWC

185

7a) The above form and method of payment are understood to be of the essence of this agreement. The ARTIST shall not perform if ARTIST has not received any and all outstanding compensation, balances or monies as stated in the deposit scheduled listed above. In the event that payments are not made as herein provided, ARTIST shall at its option, have the right to refuse to perform and PURCHASER shall remain liable to ARTIST for the agreed price herein set forth.

ADDITIONAL TERMS AND CONDITIONS

MARTINEZ, MORGALO & ASSOCIATES. Acts solely as an agent for Artist(s) herein and it is understood by purchaser that may in no way be held responsible for non-performance, lateness or any other action by Artist(s) which interfere with performance of this agreement.

Any musician hired to perform on this agreement is free to cease service hereunder by reason of any strike, ban, and unfair list, order of requirement of Local 802 of the American Federation of Musicians. The agreement of the musicians to perform is further subject to proven inability due to sickness, accidents, or accidents by means of transportation, riots, strikes, epidemics, acts of God, or any other legitimate conditions beyond the control of the musicians.

In the event the employer fails, neglects or refuses to pay the wage or other payments agreed upon herein and suit is commenced to recover the aforesaid or any part thereof, the employer shall be responsible for the attorney's fees, court costs and expenses incurred in recovery of the sums due.

Purchaser shall pay and hold ARTIST harmless of and free of and from any and all taxes, fees, dues and the like to the engagement hereunder and the sums payable to the ARTIST shall be free of such taxes, fees, dues and the like.

ALL advertising and artwork is subject to the approval of
MARTINEZ, MORGALO & ASSOCIATES

NOTE: ANY CANCELLATION BY PURCHASER WILL RESULT IN FORFEIT OF DEPOSIT.

MARTINEZ, MORGALO &
ASSOCIATES
F/S/O RUBEN BLADES &
WILLIE COLON
Print Leaders Name

DISSAR Production
ARIEL RIVAS
Print Employers Name

Paseo Degetau 2504
Caguas PR

ARTURO MARTINEZ - AGENT
Agent

Address

(787) 747 3546 Tel.
(787) 747 3506 Fax.
Telephone (Home & Business)

0026

APPENDIX E

Siembra Contract
Version # 2

Case 3:07-cv-01380-BJM   Document 285-9   Filed 10/06/11   Page 1 of 2

Deposit Received	Date Received

Martinez, Morgalo & Associates
Suite 601

New York, NY 10038
TEL. 212 349-4001
FAX 212 349-4002
E-MAIL. Arturo@martinezmorgalo.com

ENGAGEMENT CONTRACT

THIS CONTRACT is for the personal services of artist on the engagement described below made this 22nd day of January 2003 between the undersigned Purchaser of Music, (herein called employer) and artist.

1) Name of Artist: RUBEN BLADES & WILLIE COLON

2) Billing Agreement: 100% SOLE TOP BILLING ON ALL FORMS OF ADVERTISING AND PROMOTIONS

3) Name and Address of Place of Engagement:
ESTADIO HIRAM BITHORN
SAN JUAN, PUERTO RICO

4) Date, Starting and Finishing time of engagement.
SATURDAY MAY 3RD, 2003
ONE CONCERT PERFORMANCE
OF MINIMUM 2 ½ HOURS
STARTING TIME AT TBD

5) Type of engagement: CONCERT

6) Wage agreed upon: $350,000.00 U.S. DOLLARS GUARANTEE, ALL- INCLUSIVE EXCEPT FOR SOUND & LIGHTS.

7) Employer will make payment as follows. 1ST DEPOSIT IN THE AMOUNT OF $62,500.00, U.S. DOLLARS RECEIVED APRIL 2002.
2ND DEPOSIT OF $112,500.00 U.S. DOLLARS GUARANTEE SHALL BE PAID, NO LATER THAN FEB 2ND, 2003
3RD DEPOSIT OF $87,500.00 U.S DOLLARS GUARANTEE SHALL BE PAID, NO LATER THAN MARCH 22ND, 2003
BALANCE OF $87,500.00 U.S. DOLLARS GUARANTEE SHALL BE PAID, NO LATER THAN APRIL 19TH, 2003.
ALL PAYMENTS MUST BE MADE IN THE FORM OF WIRE TRANFER, CASH, CERTIFIED CHECK OR MONEY ORDER PAYABLE TO MARTINEZ, MORGALO AND ASSOCIATES. (ARTIST MUST RECEIVE PAYMENT IN FULL 14 DAYS PRIOR TO DEPARTURE FOR PUERTO RICO)

07-1360
DEPOSITION
EXHIBIT
B
L. J. Wrangler
22-04-09

EXHIBIT

Martinez 7

7a) The above form and method of payment are understood to be of the essence of this agreement. The ARTIST shall not perform if ARTIST has not received any and all outstanding compensation, balances or monies as stated in the deposit scheduled listed above. In the event that payments are not made as herein provided, ARTIST shall at its option, have the right to refuse to perform and PURCHASER shall remain liable to ARTIST for the agreed price herein set forth.

ADDITIONAL TERMS AND CONDITIONS

MARTINEZ, MORGALO & ASSOCIATES. Acts solely as an agent for Artist(s) herein and it is understood by purchaser that may in no way be held responsible for non-performance, lateness or any other action by Artist(s) which interfere with performance of this agreement

Any musician hired to perform on this agreement is free to cease service hereunder by reason of any strike, ban, and unfair list, order of requirement of Local 802 of the American Federation of Musicians The agreement of the musicians to perform is further subject to proven inability due to sickness, accidents, or accidents by means of transportation, riots, strikes, epidemics, acts of God, or any other legitimate conditions beyond the control of the musicians

In the event the employer fails, neglects or refuses to pay the wage or other payments agreed upon herein and suit is commenced to recover the aforesaid or any part thereof, the employer shall be responsible for the attorney's fees, court costs and expenses incurred in recovery of the sums due

Purchaser shall pay and hold ARTIST harmless of and free of and from any and all taxes, fees, dues and the like to the engagement hereunder and the sums payable to the ARTIST shall be free of such taxes, fees, dues and the like.

ALL advertising and artwork is subject to the approval of
MARTINEZ, MORGALO & ASSOCIATES

NOTE: ANY CANCELLATION BY PURCHASER WILL RESULT IN FORFEIT OF DEPOSIT.

	MARTINEZ, MORGALO & ASSOCIATES F/S/O RUBEN BLADES & WILLIE COLON
DISSAR Production ARIEL RIVAS	Print Leaders Name
Print Employers Name	
Signature of Employer	Signature of Leader
Paseo Degetau 2504 Caguas PR	
	ARTURO MARTINEZ - AGENT
Address	Agent
(787) 747 3546 Tel. (787) 747 3506 Fax. Telephone (Home & Business)	

APPENDIX F

Siembra Contract

Version # 3

Deposit Received	Date Received

Martinez, Morgalo & Associates
64 Fulton Street
Suite 601
New York, NY 10038
TEL. 212 349-4001
FAX 212 349-4002
E-MAIL. Arturo@martinezmorgalo.com

ENGAGEMENT CONTRACT

THIS CONTRACT is for the personal services of artist on the engagement described below made this 22nd day of **January 2003** between the undersigned Purchaser of Music, (herein called employer) and artist.

1)   Name of Artist: **RUBEN BLADES & WILLIE COLON**

2)   Billing Agreement: **100% SOLE TOP BILLING ON ALL FORMS OF ADVERTISING AND PROMOTIONS**

3)   Name and Address of Place of Engagement: **ESTADIO HIRAM BITHORN SAN JUAN, PUERTO RICO**

4)   Date, Starting and Finishing time of engagement: **SATURDAY MAY 3RD, 2003 ONE CONCERT PERFORMANCE OF MINIMUM 2 ½ HOURS STARTING TIME AT TBD**

5)   Type of engagement: **CONCERT**

6)   Wage agreed upon: **$350,000.00 U.S. DOLLARS GUARANTEE, ALL- INCLUSIVE EXCEPT FOR SOUND & LIGHTS.**

7)   Employer will make payment as follows: 1ST **DEPOSIT IN THE AMOUNT OF $62,500.00, U.S. DOLLARS RECEIVED APRIL 2002.**
2ND **DEPOSIT OF $112,500.00 U.S. DOLLARS GUARANTEE SHALL BE PAID, NO LATER THAN FEB 22ND, 2003**
3RD **DEPOSIT OF $87,500.00 U.S DOLLARS GUARANTEE SHALL BE PAID, NO LATER THAN MARCH 22ND, 2003**
BALANCE OF $87,500.00 U.S. DOLLARS GUARANTEE SHALL BE PAID, NO LATER THAN APRIL 19TH, 2003,
ALL PAYMENTS MUST BE MADE IN THE FORM OF WIRE TRANFER, CASH, CERTIFIED CHECK OR MONEY ORDER PAYABLE TO MARTINEZ, MORGALO AND ASSOCIATES. (ARTIST MUST RECEIVE PAYMENT IN FULL 14 DAYS PRIOR TO DEPARTURE FOR PUERTO RICO)

7a) The above form and method of payment are understood to be of the essence of this agreement. The ARTIST shall not perform if ARTIST has not received any and all outstanding compensation, balances or

EXHIBIT
4

monies as stated in the deposit scheduled listed above. In the event that payments are not made as herein provided, ARTIST shall at its option, have the right to refuse to perform and PURCHASER shall remain liable to ARTIST for the agreed price herein set forth.

ADDITIONAL TERMS AND CONDITIONS

MARTINEZ, MORGALO & ASSOCIATES. Acts solely as an agent for Artist(s) herein and it is understood by purchaser that may in no way be held responsible for non-performance, lateness or any other action by Artist(s) which interfere with performance of this agreement.

Any musician hired to perform on this agreement is free to cease service hereunder by reason of any strike, ban, and unfair list, order of requirement of Local 802 of the American Federation of Musicians. The agreement of the musicians to perform is further subject to proven inability due to sickness, accidents, or accidents by means of transportation, riots, strikes, epidemics, acts of God, or any other legitimate conditions beyond the control of the musicians.

In the event the employer fails, neglects or refuses to pay the wage or other payments agreed upon herein and suit is commenced to recover the aforesaid or any part thereof, the employer shall be responsible for the attorney's fees, court costs and expenses incurred in recovery of the sums due.

Purchaser shall pay and hold ARTIST harmless of and free of and from any and all taxes, fees, dues and the like to the engagement hereunder and the sums payable to the ARTIST shall be free of such taxes, fees, dues and the like.

ALL advertising and artwork is subject to the approval of
MARTINEZ, MORGALO & ASSOCIATES

NOTE: ANY CANCELLATION BY PURCHASER WILL RESULT IN FORFEIT OF DEPOSIT.

ROMPEOLA **CESAR SAINZ**	DISSAR RECORDS **ARIEL RIVAS**	MARTINEZ, MORGALO & ASSOCIATES F/S/O RUBEN BLADES
Print Employers Name		Print Leaders Name
Signature of Employer Rompeolas Calle hija del Caribe #208 2do piso Hato Rey, PR 00918 (787) 753 8244 Tel. (787) 787 3140 Fax.	Signature of Employer Dissar Degetau # 2504, PR 00727 (787) 747-3546 tel (787) 747-3596 fax	Signature of Leader ARTURO MARTINEZ - AGENT

Appendix G

Email from Arturo to Willie Colón Confirming Concert Date
dated Jan 20 2003

Subj: **Saludos...**
Date: 1/20/2003 7:00:06 PM Eastern Standard Time
From: Martinezmorgalo
To:

Hi Willie,
      I hope upon receipt of this message all is well. Willie below is a list of songs Ruben checked off. I know you sent me 5 songs you already have, but can you check off which of the following songs you have arrangements for?

      On another note I was explaining to Mrs. Colon that most of the venues are requesting dates in July/August (Gives us more time to prepare) due to the magnitude of the show and larger venues. The one show we have pending is for Puerto Rico on the 3rd of May, Mrs. Colon said the date seemed OK. We are about to lock in the show (I have to get an estimate on all expenses * all-inclusive show*) and I just wanted to confirm the date was open.

      Please highlight which tune you have, and the rest I will have trasnscribed. Thanks agin. Have a great day.

_Arturo

1. Metiendo Mano
2. Pablo Pueblo
3. Segun el color
4. La maleta
5. Me recordaras
6. Plantacion adentro
7. La mora
8. Lluvia de tu cielo
9. Pueblo
10. Plastico - Done
11. Buscando guayaba - Done
12. Pedro navaja - Done
13. Maria lionza
14. Ojos - Done
15. Dime
16. Manuela
17. El nacimiento de ramiro
18. Manuela despues
19. Maestra vida
20. Tiburon
21. Te estan buscando
22. Madam kalalu
23. El telefonito
24. Ligia Elena - Done
25. De que?
26. Yo puedo vivir del amor
27. What happened
28. Lo pasado no perdona
29. El Cazanguero
30. Juana Pena
31. Barrunto
32. Ghana E
33. Che Che cole
34. Te Conozco Bacalao
35. Jazzy
36. Auscencia
37. Calle Luna, Calle Sol

Thursday, January 23, 2003 America Online: Martinezmorgalo

Decisiones

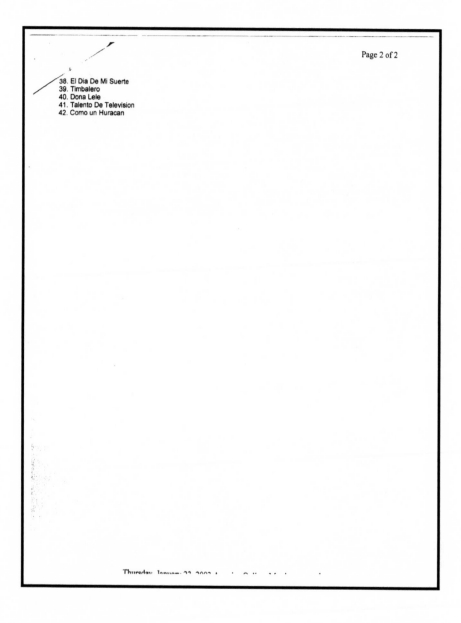

38. El Dia De Mi Suerte
39. Timbalero
40. Dona Lele
41. Talento De Television
42. Como un Huracan

Thursday, January 23, 2003

Appendix H
Proposal for *Siembra* Concert from Promoter to Arturo dated Jan 21 2003

CERTIFIED TRANSLATION   by: Olga M. Alicea, fcci, njitc-s

1/21/2003

Dear Arturo:

Receive cordial greetings, we take this opportunity to refer to several points connected with the Rubén Blades and Willie Colón show in Puerto Rico next May 3 of this year.

1. It is extremely important to us to begin the promotion at least 3 months in advance or better yet, as of next February 3 (this being the promotion standard for shows in the Hiram Bighorn stadium, for example: Shakira began being advertised in December and the show is in March, shows like those of Juan Luis Guerra, Marc Anthony, Alejandro Sanz, Luis Miguel, etc., are always advertised at least 3 months in advance.

2. With respect to promotion, radio station Salsoul is the one that has opened its doors to support the show since the beginning with the following offer:
   a. Only 30 days promotion
   b. 30 second spots
   c. 8 spots daily
   d. Pay 50% of the promotion cost in money and the other 50% in tickets to the concert.
   They mentioned to Cesar that the station's rules do not allow promoting a show for more than 30 days.

We respect the bonds that link Rubén with National Salsa Day and we enjoyed his magnificent presentation last year together with Editus. However, the possibility of presenting Rubén again this year conflicts with the promotion that we need to give to the show. This for the reasons specified before and in addition because:

1. Z93 does not do joint promotions of another event with National Salsa Day, therefore, we would have approximately 45 days to promote Rubén's show.

2. Our first option to promote the event as of today is SalSoul.
   Competition Z93

Arturo:
- We have been working with the possibility of presenting Rubén in Puerto Rico since 2001, when we made the first approach to Rubén personally in Los Angeles at a Grammy's homage of Paul Simon, where he referred us to you and we were able to commence negotiations within which the Dominican Republic was closed.
- We have complied with the corresponding deposits to Rubén's show punctually and whenever you requested it of us, the case being that you already have the first $62,500 that we sent some months ago.
- In other words, we have worked approximately a year and a half for this project to be a reality, and making clear our interest and perseverance in this concert.
- We are sure that we can find a favorable solution for all, within which we present (2) proposals for your consideration.

Translation page 6 of 17

CERTIFIED TRANSLATION   by: Olga M. Alicea, fcci, njitc-s

- First Proposal:
  - ○ Get through you directly Z93 to give us promotion for a minimum of 2 and a half months.
  - ○ That the promotion be together with that of National Salsa Day, with the same offer as Salsoul.
  - ○ If Rubén participates in National Salsa Day, that it not be announced, but that it be a surprise.
  - ○ That the artists' cache be three hundred thousand dollars; this way we will be able to purchase promotion at other stations and reinforce the promotion.

- Second Proposal:
  - ○ Carry out the event with SalSoul only, aware that this would imply Rubén not participating in National Salsa Day.

Arturo, honestly, we can meet with you and with Rubén whether in New York or in Los Angeles to present this to you personally and reach the best agreement possible.

Since Puerto Rico is the first concert of this fabulous tour, we must concentrate all our energies in this being a resounding success and not deviate our efforts in other activities not connected with Rubén's and Willie's concert, knowing that the eyes of all of the other countries where they are going to appear will be watching what happens in Puerto Rico.

Arturo, once more, thank you for all your support with this project, and we hope to have news from you as soon as possible.

Sincerely,

Ariel Rivas and Cesar Sainz.

1/21/2003

Estimado Arturo.

Recibe un cordial saludo, aprovechamos la presente para hacer referencia a varios puntos relacionados al show de Rubén Blades y Willie Colón en Puerto Rico el próximo 3 de Mayo del presente año

1. Es para nosotros de suma importancia comenzar la promoción por lo menos con 3 meses de anticipación o mejor dicho a partir del 3 de febrero próximo (siendo este el estándar de promoción para shows en el estadio Hiram Bithorn, a modo de ejemplo. Shakira se comenzó a anunciar en diciembre y el show es en marzo, shows como los de Juan Luis Guerra, Marc Anthony, Alejandro Sanz, Luis Miguel ,etc. Siempre se han anunciado por lo menos con 3 meses de anticipación

2. En cuanto a promoción la radio emisora salsoul es la que nos ha abierto sus puerta para apoyar el show desde un principio con la siguiente oferta.
   a. 3 meses de promoción
   b. Pautas de 60 segundos
   c. 16 pautas diarias
   d. Toda la promoción sin costo

3. Cesar en el mes de Noviembre del año pasado se reunió con el presidente y el vice-presidente de Z93 los cuales estuvieron interesados en promocionar a Rubén bajo las siguientes condiciones.
   a. Solo 30 días de promoción
   b. Pautas de 30 segundos
   c. 8 pautas diarias
   d. Pagar el 50% del costo de la promoción con dinero y el otro 50% en boletos para el concierto
   Ellos le mencionaron a Cesar que las reglas de la emisora no permiten promocionar un espectáculo más de 30 días

Respetamos los lazos que unen a Rubén con el día nacional de la salsa y disfrutamos de su magnifica presentación el año pasado junto a Editus Sin embargo la posibilidad de que Rubén se presente nuevamente este año, configle con la promoción que necesitamos darle al show. Esto por las razones especificadas anteriormente y además por:

1. Z93 no hace promoción conjunta de otro evento con el día nacional de la salsa, por lo tanto solo tendríamos aproximadamente 45 días de promoción para el show de Rubén

2. Nuestra primera   opción para promocionar el evento al día de hoy es SalSoul Competencia z93

Arturo:

- Hemos venido trabajando con la posibilidad de presentar a Rubén en Puerto Rico desde el 2001, donde le hicimos el primer acercamiento a Rubén personalmente en los Ángeles en un homenaje de los Grammys a Paul Simon, donde nos refirió contigo y pudimos comenzar negociaciones dentro de las cuales se cerró República Dominicana

- Hemos cumplido con los depósitos correspondientes al show de Rubén puntualmente y en los momentos que ustedes los han requerido, dándose el caso de que ya ustedes cuentan con los primeros $ 62,500 dólares que enviamos desde hace varios meses.

- En otras palabras hemos trabajado aproximadamente año y medio para que este proyecto sea una realidad, y dejando claro nuestro interés y perseverancia en este concierto

- Estamos seguros de que podemos encontrar una solución favorable para todos Dentro de las cuales planteamos (2) propuestas a su consideración.

Martinez 2

- Primera Propuesta:
  - o Conseguir por medio de ustedes directamente que Z93 nos de la promoción por un mínimo de 2 meses y medio
  - o Que la promoción sea conjunta con la del día nacional de la salsa. Con la misma oferta de Salsoul
  - o En el caso de que Rubén participe en el día nacional de la salsa que no sea anunciado si no una sorpresa
  - o Que el caché de los artistas sea de trescientos mil dólares; para nosotros de esta manera poder comprar promoción en otras emisoras y reforzar la promoción.

- Segunda Propuesta:
  - o Realizar el evento con SalSoul únicamente, conscientes de que esto implicaría la no participación de Rubén en el día Nacional de la Salsa.

Arturo, con toda confianza podemos reunirnos contigo y con Rubén ya sea en New York o en los Angeles para plantearles esto personalmente y llegar al mejor acuerdo posible

Siendo Puerto Rico el primer concierto de esta fabulosa gira debemos concentrar todas nuestras energías en que este sea un éxito rotundo y no desviar nuestros esfuerzos en otras actividades no relacionadas con el concierto de Rubén y Willie, a sabiendas de que los ojos de todos los demás países donde se van a presentar estarán pendientes de lo que ocurra en Puerto Rico.

Arturo una vez más gracias por todo tu apoyo en este proyecto y esperamos tener noticias tuyas a la brevedad posible.

Atte

Ariel Rivas y Cesar Sainz

APPENDIX I

Confirmation Letter of *Siembra* Concert from Arturo to Promoters
dated Jan 22 2003

CERTIFIED TRANSLATION   by: Olga M. Alicea, fcci, njitc-s

[MM & Associates Logo]

January 22, 2003

Mr. Cesar Sainz and Ariel Rivas
Ref. Ruben Blades and Willie Colón

Pursuant to our conversations, I hereby confirm the date of Saturday, May 3, 2003 for, the exclusive presentation of Ruben Blades and Willie Colón at the Hiram Bithorn Stadium in Puerto Rico.

Sincerely,

[Signed]

Arturo Martínez

MARTINEZ, MORGALO and ASSOCIATES, Inc.
64 FULTON STREET – SUITE 601 – NEW YORK, NY 10038 – TEL. (212) 349-4001 – FAX (212) 349 - 4002

Translation page 1 of 17

January 22, 2003

Sr. Cesar Sainz y Ariel Rivas
Ref. Ruben Blades y Willie Colon

De acuerdo a nuestra conversaciones aqui le confirmo las fecha del Sabado 3 de

Mayo del Año 2003 de la presentacion exclusivo de Ruben Blades y Willie Colon en el

Estadio Hiram Bithorn de Puerto Rico.

Atentamente,

Arturo Martinez

MARTINEZ, MORGALO and ASSOCIATES, Inc.
64 FULTON STREET • SUITE 601 • NEW YORK, NY 10038 • TEL. (212) 349-4001 • FAX. (212)349-4002
martinezmorgalo@aol.com

1 0

APPENDIX J

Letter from Rubén Blades to Willie Colón
dated May 10 2003

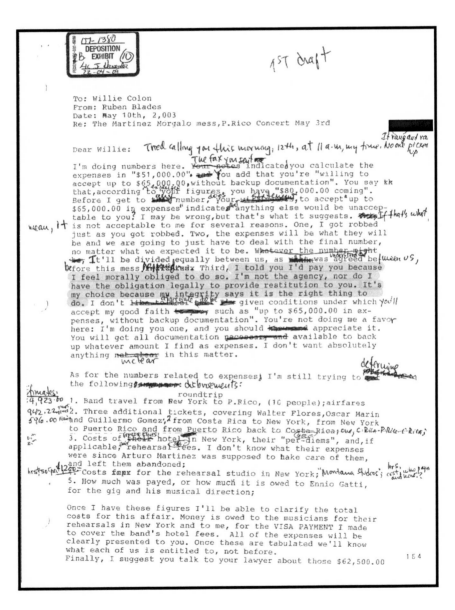

1ST draft

To: Willie Colon
From: Ruben Blades
Date: May 10th, 2,003
Re: The Martinez Morgalo mess, P.Rico Concert May 3rd

Dear Willie: Tried calling you this morning, 12th, at 11 a.m, my time. No one picked up
If Raul and Ivan
The fax you sent

I'm doing numbers here. Your notes indicated you calculate the
expenses in "$51,000.00". and You add that you're "willing to
accept up to $65,000.00,without backup documentation". You say kk
that,according to your figures, you have "$80,000.00 coming".
Before I get to any number, your ultimatum, to accept "up to
$65,000.00 in expenses" indicates anything else would be unacceptable
table to you. I may be wrong,but that's what it suggests. If that's what
it   is not acceptable to me for several reasons. One, I got robbed
mean, it   just as you got robbed. Two, the expenses will be what they will
be and we are going to just have to deal with the final number,
no matter what we expected it to be. Whatever the number might
be, It'll be divided equally between us, as was agreed before between us,
before this mess Third, I told you I'd pay you because
I feel morally obliged to do so. I'm not the agency, nor do I
have the obligation legally to provide restitution to you. It's
my choice because my integrity says it is the right thing to
do. I don't given conditions under which you'll
accept my good faith such as "up to $65,000.00 in ex-
penses, without backup documentation". You're not doing me a favor
here: I'm doing you one, and you should appreciate it.
You will get all documentation available to back
up whatever amount I find as expenses. I don't want absolutely
anything unclear in this matter.

As for the numbers related to expenses, I'm still trying to determine
the following disbursements:
                            roundtrip
estimates:
4,923.00   1. Band travel from New York to P.Rico, (10 people);airfares
942.22   2. Three additional tickets, covering Walter Flores,Oscar Marin
596.00   and Guillermo Gomez; from Costa Rica to New York, from New York
to Puerto Rico and from Puerto Rico back to Costa Rica; C.Rica-P.Rico-C.Rica;
3. Costs of their hotel in New York, their "per-diems", and,if
applicable, rehearsal fees. I don't know what their expenses
were since Arturo Martinez was supposed to take care of them,
and left them abandoned;
1240   4. Costs for for the rehearsal studio in New York; Montana Studios; hrs, who pays cost and how?;
5. How much was payed, or how much it is owed to Ennio Gatti,
for the gig and his musical direction;

Once I have these figures I'll be able to clarify the total
costs for this affair. Money is owed to the musicians for their
rehearsals in New York and to me, for the VISA PAYMENT I made
to cover the band's hotel fees. All of the expenses will be
clearly presented to you. Once these are tabulated we'll know
what each of us is entitled to, not before.
Finally, I suggest you talk to your lawyer about those $62,500.00   154

1st Draft

(2)

that the promoters claim they payed to Martinez,Morgalo. *Dos*
suggested,when we spoke, that this situation may be interpreted
as a separate transaction between them, since it involved a different arrangement,at a different time. My accountant is going
through all the deposits received by us, coming from
Martinez,Morgalo, since February of 2,002, to see if we find
anything related to this alleged payment of $62,500.00. My bank
in L.A. is doing the same. Hopefully I'll have answers by next
Friday, the 18th. There's an outside chance we may have a claim
here, since they sent a total of $287,500.00 related to the May
3rd show, not $350,000.00. Martinez Morgalo cheated them, if
they believed the $62,500.00 from 2,002 was going to be applied
to the May 3rd show as a down payment. So we'd still be owed
that amount,perhaps, from the promoters and they would have to
recoup it from Martinez,Moargz Morgalo. It might be pulling at
straws but ask your attorney. He gave me good advice before.
I hope you're reasonably well. Give my best to Julie and the
family.

As for

155

Appendix K
Letter from Rubén Blades to Willie Colón
dated May 14 2003

#12 (uc

TO: W.A.C.
FROM: R.B.
DATE: MAY 14th, 2,003
RE: THE PROBLEM,GENERAL

Dear Willie:

Tried calling you today,again, at ███████████, and couldn't
reach you. Yesterday's call, the same, so I'm faxing you with
the latest developments.

1. Arturo called me yesterday afternoon but just left his name
on my machine. I was out. Nothing new there yet.
2. I told Juan Toro to tell Arturo he must come clean in this
mess ASAP, AND THAT THIS SITUATION IS NOT GOING TO "go away".
Specifically, I'm interested in what happened with the alleged
payment of $62,500.00 made last year, for a different show, and
applied to the May 3rd engagement. I also want Arturo to clarify
the extent of Roberto Morgalo's involvement in this situation.
So far, Arturo is the one we all have focused on. But it seems
to me it's obvious Morgalo had a hand as well in the embezzlement
and it's in Arturo's personal interest to explain what role
the latter played in this.

3. Your fax of yesterday,re: P.Rico 's "Nuevo Dia" report:

Contrary to your perception, it is important for everyone, especially the Hacienda people in P.Rico, to be constantly reminded
we didn't get paid. The amount of the reported purse, $350,000.-
made a huge impact on their perception of what is owed to the
Commonwealth. We were victims here, of third parties. Note that
I assume the responsibility for the loan from Gilberto'soffice,
not you. Reports continue on this matter because it's what the
press does. I strongly suggest you put together a report on the
events so that you can present it to Hacienda, in due time.
They gave me until June 15th to do so. They were not pleased by
the promoters decision not to retain the percentage they were
supposed to withhld withhold for the local Treasury, nor with
the fact that you were not present at the meeting I had with
them. You have a valid reason: you had a show next day in Florida. Make sure to state that in your report to them. As for the
percentage question related to the promoters, that's their problem to explain. The performance we gave on the May 3rd show in
no way is affected by the fact we got ripped off. On the contrary, it makes it even bigger, since we played for the people and
to defend our reputations, as musicians and professionals, not
just for the money,(it was gone mostly).

4. I'm concerned about your statement in the May 8th fax you
sent me, when you wrote," I estimate our expenses to be approximately $51,000.00 but I'm willing to accept UP TO $65,000.00
without back-up documentation. According to my figures, I have
$80,000.00 coming". This suggest that anything else would be
unacceptable to you. I don't appreciate this, if it is what it
sounds like. I got robbed too. The expenses will be what they

(2)

are, not what we expect them to be. I've spent all of these days
going through all of the numbers, receipts and figures, on my
own account, to make everything cristal-clear to all parties involved. There were expenses, like those of Walter Flores and
Guillermo Gomez, that were not reported before. They were in New
York from April 26th until the day they left for Puerto Rico,
and I had to track them down in Costa Rica first, and then ask
Juan Toro to provide me with the hotel receipt from New York.
The point is, I will provide all back-up documentation available,
as it is provided to me, and you will have a total of expenses.
Once that is established, your fee will be determined, as well
as mine. With Puerto Rico's Hacienda, or with the I.R.S. HERE,
I don't want any unclear scenarios. I trust you know I'm not now
going to try to rip you off. I don't have to do this legally, but
morally, and that's my intent.

5. Talk to your attorney, Das, and see what he thinks of the missing $62,500.00 the promoters claim was applied, from another
show, to the May 3rd event. He mentioned something about it,
when we spoke and he advised the wisdom of doing the gig. It was
sound advise. Maybe he has more to say on this other issue?

I have my in-laws here, visiting, and it is tough to do all of the
things I need to do and take care of them, (they're elderly folks)
As soon as possible, I'll send you all the numbers. For the time
being, I instructed Juan Toro to pay the $2,700.00 owed to the
New York-based musicians for the rehearsals, and the $2,000.00
owed to Ennio Gatti. I'll send Juan a personal check for the total, $4,700.00, this week. Juan spoke to Irizarry about it, or
so he told me. Each musician will be paid separately, as Iriza-
rry suggested.
I regret this whole situation and I'm trying to clarify it and to
resolve it asap. Please, be patient. As for Arturo and Morgalo:
the only reason I have waited before going through with a criminal action against them is that we need to understand what was
the final amount stolen. This can only be determined AFTER all
expenses are clearly established. The amount missing will be the
amount misappropiated by their office. On this basis then a claim
can be presented against them. Also, the only way this amount can
ever be repayed, as far as I can see, is if they agree to do so,
and the only way for them to do this is by working to pay their
debt. Don't know how, but the other option is sending them to
jail and that doesn't really help anyone, in my opinion.
I need a mailing address to send you my report on expenses, etc,
as faxes can beunclear. Give my best to Julie and kids.
Un abrazo, Ruben

Report on expenses for the May 3rd show

As of May 16th

A. RECEIVED BY WILLIE COLON AND RUBEN BLADES: $180,460.00

a.) Wire transfers to Willie Colon: total,$62,500.00
b.) Wire transfers to Ruben Blades: total,$68,125.00 X MAY 16th
c.) Wire transfer of M&M balance left: $49,835.00

                                TOTAL: $180,460.00

B. Expenses: by MARTINEZ & MORGALO: $44,006.80
(it includes their 10%Commh)

    Expenses: paid by Colon/Blades: $29,000.75

    TOTAL OF EXPENSES,TO MAY 16th ($73,007.55)

C. Total of money accounted for: $180,460.00 (received)
                                 $ 44,006.80 (spent M&M)

    TO MAY 16th,   TOTAL: $224,466.80

D. AMOUNT CONTRACTED: $350,000.00

E. AMOUNT UNACCOUNTED FOR: $125,533.20

AMOUNT STOLEN IN 2,002:* $62,500.00
AMOUNT STOLEN IN 2,003: $63,033.20

* The amount the promoters claim they payed in 2,002 for a
show I was to do and that was cancelled (twice) by them due
to"conflicting schedules". The promoters claim M & M accepted
to credit this $62,500.00 as a payment against the $350,000.00
for a new show (Willie Colon & Ruben Blades, on May 3rd),2,003.
This was never mentioned to Willie Colon or to Ruben Blades
and it doesn't appear in the contract presented to Willie Colon
by M & M regarding the May 3rd date.

102

Chronology

May 21, 2002
- $12,500 "good faith" deposit (10%) paid by Rompeolas (Arial Rivas) for Rubén Blades' December concert.

May 30, 2002
- Rubén Blades' December concert contract drafted.

June 7, 2002
- Full deposit of $62,500 for Rubén Blades' December concert was due but not received.

June 27, 2002
- Second deposit ($20,000) for Rubén Blades' December concert paid by Rompeolas / Cesar Sainz (Arial Rivas).

October 3, 2002
- Third deposit ($20,000) for Rubén Blades' December concert paid by Rompeolas / Cesar Sainz (Arial Rivas).

October 29, 2002
- Final deposit ($10,000) for Rubén Blades' December concert paid by Rompeolas / Cesar Sainz (Arial Rivas).

  NOTE: Total deposits for December concert equal $62,500.

December 7, 2002
- Rubén Blades' December concert officially cancelled.

December 10, 2002
- Wire transfer #1 for $25,000 from Martinez, Morgalo & Associates to Rubén Blades Productions for cancelled December concert.
- Wire transfer #2 for $25,000 from Martinez, Morgalo & Associates to Rubén Blades Productions for cancelled December concert.

January 14-16, 2003
- Robert Morgalo at military training in Fort Indian Town Gap, PA.

January 16, 2003
- Received warning order (WARNO) to report for active duty.
- Robert Morgalo resigns as CEO of Martinez, Morgalo & Associates.

January 16-21, 2003
- Robert Morgalo reports to Army Reserves unit to prepare for deployment.

January 18, 2003
- Surprise birthday and going-away party at Robert Morgalo's home.

January 20, 2003
- E-mail from Arturo Martinez to Willie Colón regarding availability for May 3rd event.

January 21, 2003
- Robert Morgalo's birthday when he reports for active duty.
- Proposal Letter from Ariel Rivas to Arturo Martinez regarding *Siembra* concert.

January 22, 2003
- *Siembra* concert confirmation from Arturo Martinez to Ariel Rivas and Cesar Sainz.
- The first, second, and third drafts of the *Siembra* concert contract were drafted and dated all on the same day by Arturo Martinez or possibly Ariel Rivas.

February 27, 2003
- First *Siembra* concert deposit paid: $72,500 by Dissar Productions / Ariel Rivas.

March 7, 2003
- Second *Siembra* concert deposit paid: $15,000 by Dissar Productions / Ariel Rivas.
- Wire Transfer from Martinez, Morgalo & Associates to Rubén Blades Productions $28,125 for *Siembra* concert.
- Wire Transfer from Martinez, Morgalo & Associates to El Malo, Inc. / Willie Colón $31,250 for *Siembra* concert.

March 25, 2003
- Third *Siembra* concert deposit paid: $60,000 by Dissar Productions / Ariel Rivas.

March 28, 2003
- Forth *Siembra* concert deposit paid: $20,000 by Dissar Productions / Ariel Rivas.
- Wire Transfer from Martinez, Morgalo & Associates to El Malo, Inc. / Willie Colón $31,250 for *Siembra* concert.

April 8, 2003
- Fifth *Siembra* concert deposit paid: $7,500 by Dissar Productions / Ariel Rivas.

April 22, 2003
- Sixth *Siembra* concert deposit paid: $25,000 by Dissar Productions / Ariel Rivas.

April 24, 2003
- Seventh *Siembra* concert deposit paid: $10,000 by Dissar Productions / Ariel Rivas.

April 29, 2003
- Eighth *Siembra* concert deposit paid: $25,000 by Dissar Productions / Ariel Rivas.
- Arturo Martinez attempts suicide. Hospitalized for 10 days.

April 30, 2003
- Final *Siembra* concert deposit paid (three days before the *Siembra* concert): $52,500 by Dissar Productions / Ariel Rivas.
- Wire Transfer from Martinez, Morgalo & Associates to Rubén Blades Productions $40,000 for *Siembra* concert.
  NOTE: Total Siembra concert deposits equal $287,500, not the contracted amount of $350,000.00. The difference is $62,500.

May 3, 2003

- *Siembra* concert with Rubén Blades and Willie Colón takes place.

May 5, 2003

- Juan Toro was given access to Martinez, Morgalo & Associates bank accounts. According to Rubén Blades, $49,835 was paid to him from the bank account funds.

May 10, 2003

- A letter from Rubén Blades was sent to Willie Colón regarding Rubén paying Willie.
- A letter from Ariel Rivas was sent to Rubén Blades regarding how deposits were made.

August 22, 2003

- Arturo Martinez goes to prison.

July 3, 2004

- Robert Morgalo returns from deployment.

The Legal Battle

May 4, 2007

- Willie Colón files lawsuit against Rubén Blades in Puerto Rico.

May 7 or 8, 2007

- Rubén Blades at press conference in Panama.

April 22, 2008

- Arturo Martinez' first deposition held at the D. Ray James Correctional Facility in Folkston, GA.

May 1, 2008

- Robert Morgalo files defamation lawsuit against Rubén Blades and Rubén Blades Productions, Inc. in the Southern District of New York.

June 5, 2008

- Rubén Blades files a cross-claim against Robert Morgalo in the Puerto Rico case.

August 8, 2008

- Robert Morgalo's defamation case against Rubén Blades was transferred from New York and consolidated with the Puerto Rico case.

October 23, 2008
- Arturo Martinez released from prison.

April 21, 2009
- Willie Colón's deposition in Puerto Rico.

April 22, 2009
- Rubén Blades' first deposition in Puerto Rico.

February 26, 2010
- Ariel Rivas' deposition held in the offices of Juan Saavedra Castro in Puerto Rico.

March 31, 2010
- Defamation case against Rubén Blades dismissed by Judge Justo Arenas.

April 5, 2010
- Default Hearing before Judge Justo Arenas at the Federal Court of Puerto Rico.

May 6, 2010
- Willie Colón voluntarily dismisses his case against Rubén Blades, Robert Morgalo, and Martinez, Morgalo & Associates, Inc.

May 17, 2010
- Trial of Rubén Blades cross-claim against Robert Morgalo begins and ends when Rubén requests to open discovery and use documents they previously asked the court to deny Robert to use at trial.

May 18, 2010
- Arturo Martinez' second deposition held in the offices of Juan Fronteras and Israel Alicea.

May 19, 2010
- Rubén Blades' second deposition in the offices of Juan Fronteras and Israel Alicea.

May 20, 2010
- Robert Morgalo's deposition held in the offices of Pamela Gonzalez in Puerto Rico.

October 21, 2010
- Court rules that Rubén Blades has no standing to sue Robert Morgalo.

November 17, 2010
- Robert Morgalo makes first public statement to the press.

Decisiones

December 7, 2010
- Robert Morgalo makes an offer to Rubén Blades for all parties to drop all litigation and just walk away with no money.

December 10, 2010
- Rubén Blades turns down offer from Robert Morgalo.

December 28, 2010
- Rubén Blades loses his motion for summary judgment against Robert Morgalo.

December 27, 2011
- Robert Morgalo wins his motion for summary judgment against Rubén Blades.

February 27, 2012
- Robert Morgalo wins appeal. 1st Circuit Court of Appeal rules that Judge Justo Arenas abused his discretion.

February 9, 2013
- Pre-trial mediation conference takes place.

February 11, 2013
- Defamation trial begins.

May 16, 2013
- Defamation case is dismissed.

Notes

All documents cited in this book
can be found on Robert Morgalo's websites:

decisionesbook.com (English) or
decisioneslibro.com (Spanish)

Chapter 1

1. Complaint, Colón v. Blades, Civ. No. 07-1380 (D.P.R. May 4, 2007), ECF No. 1.
2. Juan Zamorano, Blades apenado con demanda de Colón [Blades Saddened by Colón's Claims], (May 9, 2007), http:// latino.msn.com/entretenimiento/noticias/ articles/articlepage.aspx?cp-documentid=48.
3. Willie Colón Demandó a Rubén Blades [Willie Colón Sued Rubén Blades], People en Español, (May 17, 2007), http://peopleenespanol.com/pespanol/ articles/0,22490,1618881,00.html.
4. Complaint, Morgalo v. Blades, Civ. No. 08-4079 (S.D.N.Y. May 1, 2008), ECF No. 1.

Chapter 12
1.   Colón Dep. 93:13-15, April 21, 2009.
2.   Ibid., 94:6-8.
3.   Ibid., 94:9-13.
4.   Ibid., 90:17-25, 91:17–19.
5.   Ibid., 95:17-19.

Chapter 13
1.   Transcript of Hearing on Default at 62:2-5, Colón v. Blades, Civ. No. 07-1380 (D.P.R. April 5, 2010).

Chapter 14
1.   Letter from Ariel Rivas to Rubén Blades (May 10, 2003) (available on author's website).
2.   Transcript of Hearing on Default, supra note 10.
3.   Ibid., 64:14-25.
4.   Letter, supra note 11, at 8.
5.   Transcript of Hearing on Default, supra note 10, at 170:20–24.

Chapter 15
1.   Orders at 4, Department of the Army, Headquarters, 99th Regional Support Command, PA, M-021-0090 (January 21, 2003).
2.   Blades Dep., 218:11-12, April 22, 2009.
3.   Transcript of Bench Trial at 40:9, Morgalo v. Blades, Civ. No. 07-1380 (D.P.R. February 11, 2013), ECF No. 356.
4.   Transcript of Hearing on Default, supra note x, at 183:3-6.

Chapter 18
1.   Colón Dep., supra note 5, at 73:6–12; 134:10–12; 158:25–159:13; 240:4–6 and 15–17; 242:14–16.

Chapter 19
1.   Blades Dep., supra note 17, at 168-75.
2.   Ibid.,175–76.

Chapter 20
1.   Colón Dep., supra note 5, at 11:15–12:10.
2.   Blades Dep., supra note 17, at 168:11–16.

Chapter 21
1.   Transcript of Hearing on Default, supra note 10, at pp. 88–102, 129, 142–45.
2.   Ibid., 26: 9–12.
3.   Blades Dep. supra note 17, at 187:21-24.
4.   Transcript of Hearing on Default, supra note 26.
5.   Morgalo Dep., at 105–07, May 20, 2010.
6.   Transcript of Hearing on Default supra note, 10 at 176:17–177:7.
7.   Ibid., 53:8-14.
8.   Ibid., 182:3–24.

9. Summons on a Third-Party Complaint to Arturo Martinez, Colón v. Morgalo, Civ. No. 07-1380 (D.P.R. April 5, 2010).
10. Summons on a Third-Party Complaint to Ariel Rivas, Colón v. Morgalo, Civ. No. 07-1380 (D.P.R. April 5, 2010).
11. Motion to Strike Third-Party Complaint, Amended Third-Party Complaint and Informative Motion pursuant to Rule 14(A) and Rule 12(f), Colón v. Blades, Civ. No. 07-1380 (D.P.R. April 7, 2010), ECF. No. 160.

Chapter 22
1. Transcript of Hearing on Default, supra note 10, at 182:5–9.
2. E-mail from Pamela Gonzalez to Israel Alicea, (November 17, 2010) (on file with author).

Chapter 23
1. Colón v. Blades, Civ. No. 07-1380, 2010 WL 3490172 (D.P.R. September 2, 2010).
2. Motion for Substitution, Civ. No. 07-1380 (D.P.R. January 17, 2011), ECF. No. 265.
3. "Rubén Blades Se Desahoga." YouTube, (December 15, 2010), http://www.youtube.com/watch?v =IFOYflbu5wA
4. Supra note 33.
5. Supra note 35.
6. E-mail from Pamela Gonzalez to Israel Alicea, (December 7, 2010) (on file with author).
7. Cross-Motion for Summary Judgment against Robert Morgalo, Colón v. Blades, Civ. No. 07-1380 (D.P.R. July 13, 2010), ECF No. 234.
8. Colón v. Blades, 757 F.Supp.2d 107, 110 (D.P.R. 2010).

Chapter 24
1. Colón v. Blades, 914 F.Supp.2d 181, 189 (D.P.R. 2011).
2. Ibid.
3. Ibid., 190.
4. Ibid., 191.
5. Ibid., 192.
6. Ibid., 193.

Chapter 25
1. Morgalo v. Blades, No. 10-1706, slip op. at 2 (1st Cir. February 27, 2012).
2. "Rubén Blades en Corte Entrevista Exclusiva con Javier Ceriani." YouTube, (February 12, 2013) https://youtu.be/nE0eioQ8SeA (this video references the video mentioned; when the mentioned video is retrieved, it will be available on the website).
3. Arturo Tito Martinez, Facebook (April 1, 2012), https://www.facebook.com/ (on file with author).

Chapter 27
1. Transcript of Bench Trial, supra note 18, at 27:3–5.
2. Zamarano, supra note 2.
3. Transcript of Bench Trial, supra note 18, at 33:11-34:18.

Chapter 28

1. Ibid., at 69:14–15.
2. Ibid., at 96:20–21.
3. Ibid., at 102:13–16.
4. Ibid., at 105:6-106:13.

Chapter 29

1. Ibid., 129:1-5.
2. Ibid., 142:5-143:6.
3. Ibid., 133:2–20.
4. Ibid., 140:22–24.
5. Ibid., 149:19-150:3; 155:23-156:1, 6–10.
6. Ibid.,158:24.
7. New York Department of State, Division of Corporations, State Records, and UCC, http://www.dos.ny.gov/corps/bus_entity_search.html; under Search Criteria field for Business Entity Name, enter "The Relentless Agency."

Chapter 30

1. Transcript of Bench Trial, supra note 18, 118:16, 121:9-12, 141:2-22.
2. Ibid., 10:19–21.
3. "Tribunal Federal Desestima Caso de Difamación contra Rubén Blades," rubenblades.com (May 20, 2013) http://rubenblades.com/rb/2013/5/26/tribunal-federal-desestima-caso-de-difamacion-contra-ruben-b.html (last visited March 10, 2016).